BEGOTTEN
OR MADE?

D0074506

BEGOTTEN OR MADE?

OLIVER O'DONOVAN

CLARENDON PRESS · OXFORD
1984

Oxford University Press, Walton Street, Oxford OX2 6DP

London New York Toronto
Delhi Bombay Calcutta Madras Karachi
Kuala Lumpur Singapore Hong Kong Tokyo
Nairobi Dar es Salaam Cape Town
Melbourne Auckland

and associated companies in
Beirut Berlin Ibadan Mexico City Nicosia

Oxford is a trade mark of Oxford University Press

Published in the United States
by Oxford University Press, New York

© Oliver O'Donovan 1984

All rights reserved. No part of this publication may be reproduced,
stored in a retrieval system, or transmitted, in any form or by any means,
electronic, mechanical, photocopying, recording, or otherwise, without
the prior permission of Oxford University Press

This book is sold subject to the condition that it shall not, by way
of trade or otherwise, be lent, re-sold, hired out or otherwise circulated
without the publisher's prior consent in any form of binding or cover
other than that in which it is published and without a similar condition
including this condition being imposed on the subsequent purchaser

British Library Cataloguing in Publication Data

O'Donovan, Oliver
Begotten or made?
1. Artificial insemination,
Human — Religious aspects — Christianity
I. Title
261.5'6   BT708

ISBN 0-19-826678-2

Set by Grestun Graphics, Abingdon and printed in Great Britain by
J. W. Arrowsmith Ltd., Bristol

JESUIT - KRAUSS - McCORMICK - LIBRARY
1100 EAST 55th STREET
CHICAGO, ILLINOIS 60615

PREFACE

When the committee responsible for planning the annual
London Lectures in Contemporary Christianity invited me
to take a bioethical theme for their 1983 series, it was not
difficult to settle on the area of artificial human fertilization. The creation of a Government Committee of Inquiry
under the chairmanship of Dame Mary Warnock in 1982
produced a flurry of urgent activity as interested organiz-
ations, including the churches and other Christian bodies,
formulated their views to submit in evidence to the Committee. The questions surrounding *in vitro* fertilization
had not been extensively discussed in the British churches
before then (though the British Council of Churches document *Choices in Childlessness* had just anticipated the
Warnock rush); artificial insemination by donor, on the
other hand, had been the subject of considerable attention
two decades earlier, and some of those discussions were
now looked at again. Some attention also began to be paid
(though, as usual, not enough) to discussions from the
other side of the Atlantic Ocean. As I looked through
evidence submitted by Christian bodies to the Warnock
Committee, and compared them with writings from other
Christian sources in the last quarter-century, it seemed to
me that a consistent concern emerged. It was expressed
as clearly by those who accepted these new techniques
as by those who rejected them. It was common to Roman
Catholics, Protestants, and Jews. It arose from a caution
about the impact of technology (which is, above all, the impact of certain ways of *thinking*) on our self-understanding
as human beings. It found common expression in a distinction that constantly recurred: between the use of technique
to assist human procreation and the transformation of
human procreation into a technical operation. It was a
concern about the capacity of technology to change, not
merely the conditions of our human existence, but its
essential characteristics.

I ought perhaps to have hesitated before presuming to go over ground which had been covered with such penetrating and economical brevity by Karl Rahner, and with such passionate and detailed thoroughness by Paul Ramsey, both writing in the late sixties.[1] Nevertheless, it became clear to me as I studied discussions from medical and legal sources that the point which churches and theologians wished to make was not being heard, or, if heard, was not being well understood, even by possibly sympathetic listeners. Dr R. G. Edwards, in his Horizon Lecture on the BBC, lamented that he had found only 'confusion . . . indecision . . . changing ideas and concepts' when he sought 'inspiration . . . advice . . . and leadership' from religious sources.[2] It seemed all the more necessary, then, to give further expression, in the context of the British debate and addressing an audience of non-theologians, to the central concern on which Christians and Jews seemed to speak with some unity. And this is what I tried to do, developing the theme in my own way and letting it lead me to my own conclusions, but nevertheless concentrating on this theme, which is liable to recur in any Christian, and perhaps any Jewish contribution to the debate. That is why the reader will find so many important matters concerning AID and IVF not touched on, or only alluded to, in the following pages: the long-term freezing of embryos before replacement, for example, the use of cloning techniques, or the selection of donors of sperm or ova. And it explains why I have included a discussion of an issue which is not immediately a matter of human fertilization at all.

It is hardly necessary these days for the theologian to apologize for trespassing in an area traditionally known as 'medical ethics'. It is clear that the issues are so wideranging that the medical profession could not, even if it wished to, claim a proprietary interest in them all. We are

[1] Karl Rahner, 'The Problem of Genetic Manipulation', in *Theological Investigations* vol. 9, tr. Graham Harrison (Darton Longman & Todd, 1970). Paul Ramsey, *Fabricated Man* (Yale University Press, 1970).

[2] *The Listener*, 27 Oct., 1983, 13.

not now engaged in the traditional 'casuistry' of a professional ethic — 'What is the doctor to do when . . .' — but with questions of how society as a whole is to respond to developments which affect us all. New issues no longer arise primarily from clinical practice, but from research in the laboratory. For this reason the neologism 'bioethics' which the Americans have forged to describe our whole field of discussion is necessary, if ugly. These are not matters which belong to one profession any more. but matters of the broadest social policy. Yet it would be a mistake to think of 'bioethics' as a new intellectual discipline in which there will be a new set of trained experts — and even more of a mistake to pretend that theologians could be those experts. It is an unfinished discussion among representatives of many disciplines and none. To this discussion the theologian has a contribution to make, a contribution which will point in certain directions and make certain challenges. Yet what I had to say in these lectures was conceived as a *contribution* to the discussion, however sharply I may have thought it necessary from time to time to do the pointing and the challenging.

The medical profession, far from being excluded by this widening of the discussion, is likely to be helped by it. Like other moralists who enjoy the privilege of professional exchanges with medical practitioners, I often find them ready to admit both perplexity and discouragement about the moral aspects of their work. But what depresses them is not a multitude of difficult conscientious decisions, but an elusive sense that they have *no* decisions to make any more, that their work has been transformed by vast social changes, so that they are expected to act on the basis of presuppositions which are in tension with their traditional self-understanding but which they cannot challenge. In response to this the moralist has to adopt a more adventurous and wide-ranging approach to the discussion. He has to do more than analyse difficult 'cases of conscience'; his argument must aim at more than demonstrating that this or that practice is legitimate or illegitimate. He has to become an interpreter, who can explain how and why these decisions now come to us in these forms and present these difficulties. He has to place medical practice in its cultural setting, so that the doctor can see where his perplexity arises from and what it is really about.

The theologian has very much to gain from the exchange in his turn. In accepting the honour done to me by the invitation to deliver these lectures, I was drawn by the promise, which was made good, of an audience containing thoughtful medical people, many of them specialists in these fields. For in their profession there is still preserved a practical memory of a way of thinking about things that is not our modern way. Medicine, with its tradition of humility before the workings of the natural order and of altruistic devotion to fostering strength and health in the weak and sick, is a kind of shrine in which banished gods still claim their secret homage, the homage of a non-manipulative approach to human nature. A theologian knows, then, that medical people still guard, however uncomfortably, a tradition which should enable them to understand him. Indeed, he should recognize that it is they, rather than he, who have been its guardians through past generations of our civilization. He brings to them what is their own, an understanding of care for persons in sickness which was fashioned by practical Christian obedience. He brings it to them mediated through his own theological analysis of contemporary problems, in the hope that they will be able to repossess it and call upon it in need. If in some medical circles (not those that so courteously attended to these lectures) the theologian is regarded as the enemy, that can only be a sign that medicine is at enmity with itself; for the theologian knows nothing in this area that the Christian tradition of medicine has not itself first taught him, in practice if not in theory.

I owe an additional word of thanks to colleagues from the Church of England Board for Social Responsibility with whom I have been able to discuss these issues in the course of work under the Board's auspices. I have learned much from them. But they are not responsible for what I may have failed to learn; nor may my views be taken as an indication of what the Board may wish to contribute to the debate at a later stage.

Christ Church, Oxford
February 1984

CONTENTS

1. MEDICINE AND THE LIBERAL REVOLUTION

When the fathers of the Council of Nicaea declared, in words familiar to every Christian who recites their creed, that the only Son of God the Father was 'begotten, not made', they intended to make a simple point. The Son was 'of one being with the Father'. He was God, just as God the Father was God. And to emphasize the point they used an analogy, based upon our twofold human experience of forming things other than ourselves. That which we beget is *like* ourselves. (I shall use the word 'beget', as the ancients did, to speak of the whole human activity of procreation, and not in the modern way, meaning especially the male side of the activity.) Our offspring are human beings, who share with us one common human nature, one common human experience and one common human destiny. We do not determine what our offspring is, except by ourselves being that very thing which our offspring is to become. Just so, the fathers said, the eternal Son of God who was not made, was of the Father's *being*, not his *will*. But that which we make is *unlike* ourselves. Whether it is made of matter, like a wooden table, or of words like a lecture, or of sounds like a symphony, or of colours and shapes like a picture, or of images like an idea, it is the product of our own free determination. We have stamped the decisions of our will upon the material which the world has offered us, to form it in this way and not in that. What we 'make', then, is alien from our humanity. In that it has a human maker, it has come to existence as a human project, its being at the disposal of mankind. It is not fit to take its place alongside mankind in fellowship, for it has no place beside him on which to stand: man's will is the law of its being. That which we beget can be, and should be, our companion; but the product of our art — whatever immeasurable satisfaction and enjoyment there may be both in making it and in cherishing it — can never have the independence to be that 'other I', equal to us and differentiated from us, which we acknowledge in those who are begotten of human seed.

In making this contrast with reference to the eternal Son of God the Nicene fathers used an analogy. Like all analogies, it has its limitations. We cannot speak of 'begetting' in the divine being without making it clear what aspects of the analogy are not applicable to the life of godhead. At the same time, we cannot say that any human beings are 'begotten, not made' in the same absolute sense that we can say it of the Son of God. For all human beings begotten of other human beings are, at the same time, 'made' by God. Of no human being can it be said that he is simply 'not made', that he is at nobody's disposal, that no higher will acts as the law of his being. God's will is such a law for every human being, and every human being is at the disposal of God. Human beings, begotten of human seed, are also made; even Jesus Christ, considered simply as a human being is a 'creature' of God. Nevertheless, the ground of the analogy holds. A being who is the 'maker' of any other being is alienated from that which he has made, transcending it by his will and acting as the law of its being. To speak of 'begetting' is to speak of quite another possibility than this: the possibility that one may form another being who will share one's own nature, and with whom one will enjoy a fellowship based on radical equality.

In this book we have to speak of 'begetting' — not the eternal begetting of the godhead, but the temporal begetting of one creature by another. We have to consider the position of this human 'begetting' in a culture which has been overwhelmed by 'making' — that is to say, in a technological culture. And here we must stress a point that is often made by those who have taught us how to think about our technological culture — we may mention George Grant's *Technology and Empire*[1] and Jacques Ellul's *The Technological Society*[2] — that what marks this culture out

[1] (Anansi, Toronto, 1969.)
[2] tr. J. Wilkinson (Jonathan Cape, 1965).

most importantly, is not anything that it does, but what it thinks. It is not 'technological' because its instruments of making are extraordinarily sophisticated (though that is evidently the case), but because it thinks of everything it does as a form of instrumental making. Politics (which should surely be the most non-instrumental of activities) is talked of as 'making a better world'; love is 'building a successful relationship'. There is no place for simply *doing*. The fate of a society which sees, wherever it looks, nothing but the products of the human will, is that it fails, when it does see some aspect of human activity which is not a matter of construction, to recognize the significance of what it sees and to think about it appropriately. This blindness in the realm of thought is the heart of what it is to be a technological culture.

Nevertheless, though thought comes first, there are implications in the realm of practice too. Such a society is incapable of acknowledging the inappropriateness of technical intervention in certain types of activity. When every activity is understood as making, then every situation into which we act is seen as a raw material, waiting to have something made out of it. If there is no category in thought for an action which is not artifactual, then there is no restraint in action which can preserve phenomena which are not artificial. This imperils not only, or even primarily, the 'environment' (as we patronizingly describe the world of things which are not human); it imperils what it is to be human, for it deprives human existence itself of certain spontaneities of being and doing, spontaneities which depend upon the reality of a world which we have not made or imagined, but which simply confronts us to evoke our love, fear, and worship. Human life, then, becomes mechanized because we cannot comprehend what it means that some human activity is 'natural'. Politics becomes controlled by media of mass communication, love by analytical or counselling techniques. And begetting children becomes subject to the medical and surgical interventions which are the theme of this book.

Let us consider a platitude which we encounter at every turn. It presents itself as a truism, so obvious that it could hardly be questioned; yet, at the same time, it presents itself as an illumination, which will banish hesitations and doubts and clear up problems. This paradoxical double aspect marks it out as the axiom of a pervasive pattern of thought. When Dr R. G. Edwards in his recent Horizon Lecture on *in vitro* fertilization gave utterance to this platitude, the editor of *The Listener*, with a journalist's flair for what commands immediate attention and consent, singled the sentence out for prominent display: 'To do nothing is just as much an ethical decision to be defended as to introduce new methods of therapy.' And, of course, read in one way the point is undeniable. Any decision is *ipso facto* a decision 'to be defended'. Moral reasoning and thought are required for all our decisions, the decision to lift our hand as well as the decision to keep it in our bosom. But read in another way it says something which previous generations of Western thinkers would have denied. A decision to do nothing is not to be justified *on the same grounds* as a decision to act. A decision to do nothing is not merely a disguised decision to act by other means. There can be a *presumption* in favour of letting alone — a rebuttable presumption, certainly, but one which still acknowledges the difference between action and non-action. In medical ethics this presumption has always played a large part. *Primum non nocere*: the doctor's first obligation was *not* to act, where there was normal life and health which his action might hurt. When Dr Edwards laid the 'onus of proof' back on to those who 'wish to maintain the status quo', he apparently intended to refuse the burden of proof which traditional moral thought about medicine would have laid upon the practitioner who would intervene.

For what remains of this chapter, then, let me attempt to say something of a very general character about the position of medicine and its concern in the midst of our technological culture. These remarks, though sketchy, will provide some kind of context for the more focussed dis-

cussions in future chapters of particular technical undertakings which promise to transform our human begetting
into making.

The relation of human beings to their own bodies, we
might say, is the last frontier of nature. However much we
may surround ourselves with our artifacts, banish every
bird from the sky and every fish from the river, tidy every
blade of grass into a park with concrete paths and iron
railings, however blind we may become to the givenness of
the natural order on which our culture is erected, nevertheless, when we take off our clothes to have a bath, we
confront something as natural, as given, as completely non-
artifactual as anything in this universe: we confront our
own bodily existence. And we learn there, if nowhere
else, that to enjoy any freedom of spirit, to realize our
possibilities for action of any kind, we must cherish nature
in this place where we encounter it, we must defer to
its immanent laws, and we must plan our activities in co-
operation with them. It was the office of medicine to teach
us this lesson in ages when the limitations of technique
gave it virtually no other office. Human freedom has a
natural substrate, a presupposition. Before we can evoke
and create new beings which conform to the laws we lay
down for them by our making, we have to accept this
being according to its own laws which we have not laid
down. If, by refusing its laws and imposing our freedom
wantonly upon it, we cause it to break down, our freedom
breaks down with it. This is in fact the law of our relations
with all nature, with the climate, the soil, the animal world.
But in this particular case it is forced upon our attention,
one might think inescapably. 'No man hates his own flesh'
says Saint Paul, 'but nourishes it and cherishes it' (Eph. 5:
29). To hate one's own flesh is the limit of self-contradiction
to which our freedom tends, it is the point at which our
assertion of ourselves against nature becomes an attack
upon ourselves; and so it is equally true to say both that
no man ever hates his own flesh, and that this self-hatred
is the term to which our proud self-assertion is inevitably

drawn, just as the worshippers of Baal on Mount Carmel, according to the prophetic history, were impelled to cut themselves with knives.

What is it that draws us on to this self-contradiction? We have spoken of a tendency of 'freedom'. And in our title we speak of a 'liberal revolution', which is to say, a revolution which has at the centre of its concern the maintenance and extension of freedoms, understood in the modern and mis-leading sense as the abolition of limits which constrain and direct us. Technology derives its social significance from the fact that by it man has discovered new freedoms from necessity. The technological transformation of the modern age has gone hand in hand with the social and political quest of Western man to free himself from the necessities imposed upon him by religion, society, and nature. With-out this social quest the development of technology would have been unthinkable; without technology the liberal so-ciety as we know it would be unworkable.

Medical technique, too, has been shaped and developed with the intention of fulfilling aspirations for freedom, freedom in this case from the necessities imposed upon us by our bodily nature. But not until recently (and this fact more than anything else bears witness to the importance of Christian influence upon medical practice) has society ventured to think that medical technique ought to be used to overcome not only the necessities of disease but also necessities of health (such as pregnancy). Although liberal political thought has been a mark of Western civilization for centuries, it has taken until very recently for a radically lib-eral concept of freedom to challenge outright the Christian understanding of freedom which was expressed in medicine. A medicine which differentiated sharply between inter-fering in a healthy body and curing a sick one, as Western Christian medicine used to do, preserved an understanding of freedom which respected the constraints of health. But now the challenge is explicit. Of all the arguments which ensured the victory of liberal abortion policy in Western societies none, I think, was so influential than the one which many of us who wrote about the subject thought too crude to be taken seriously: the woman's right to self-determination in respect of her own body. The appeal to this right (conceived to be effective irrespective of whether the woman's body is healthy or sick) evoked subliminal consent even from those who professed to find it rationally empty, for it gave voice to the profoundest political commitments which underlie liberal society in the West.

Yet when we consider the abortion example we immediately face a paradox. The freedom of self-determination which was accorded to the mother was won at the cost of the physician's freedom. The attempt to entrench the physician's right of dissent in the 'conscience clause' of the 1967 Abortion Act was a notorious failure, and for rather obvious reasons. The organization of mass medicine requires predictability of performance. A hospital schedule cannot be planned around individuals who may, or may not, when it comes to it, assist at an abortion. The rule must be that if they can't stand the heat they must get out of the kitchen, and the best that can be said for the conscience clause is that it has sometimes provided a graceful mode of exit. This loss of freedom on the physician's part points us to a contradiction which lies at the heart of the phenomenon of a liberal *revolution*.

My use of this word is by no means rhetorical, merely suggesting that our period is a period of great change. Great change can happen for all kinds of reasons; but revolution happens for only one reason, and that is that a community seeks to act together *en masse* in such a way as to fashion its own future. Consider what is expressed by the phrase 'fashioning the future', and how it differs from the simple conception of 'acting together'. An action is an event which has a beginning and an end; and when one completes what one is doing, one launches it, as it were, upon the stream of history. What happens to it then is out of one's own control. *Something* will happen to it, certainly, and it will make *some* impact upon the future, because deeds have extended repercussions through their chain of consequences. Yet one cannot *perform* the consequences as one performs the deed itself. They are, as it were, a cargo of unexplored possibilities when one lets the deed slip out from under one's hand, and one must simply entrust one's bark to a course of events which one cannot rule. To act well, then, requires faith in divine providence, because one must hope (without the possibility of calculative proof) that what one has done will be used for the service of others rather than their hurt. But to 'fashion the future' is to refuse to let one's act go. It is to strive to extend one's control even to directing the stream of history, diverting it, if need be, to ensure that one's bark never strikes a rock. It is to assume a totalistic responsibility for what will happen, to treat the whole course of events as an artifact which one can mould in one's hands. 'Revolution' is a word which speaks of this assumption of responsibility by a community over its total future — a word which never entered the vocabulary of the West until faith in divine providence was weakening. The extraordinary burden which such a responsibility must impose upon one's actions is the reason why so many revolutions have been carried through with violent and crude actions. But this is not an essential feature of a revolution. Our technological revolution is in some ways more truly a revolution than any that has yet been, for it not only expresses a mass desire to mould the future in a new shape, but it has the technique which makes that project practicable.

We have to do, then, with a mass movement. The quest for freedom from natural limits is not the private campaign of a small technocratic élite. It may be true, as C. S. Lewis warned us sombrely in *The Abolition of Man*,[3] that the so-called mastery of man over himself can only turn out to mean the mastery of some men over other men. But that does not mean that the project of human self-mastery *began* as a conspiracy by a few men to master others. A criticism that might possibly be made against Lewis's

---

[3] Macmillan, 1947.

famous cautionary fable about the totalitarian pretensions of technology, *That Hideous Strength*, is that it embraces too readily the myth of the mad scientist. The mad scientist, as we all know, sits in his laboratory developing the ultimate weapon to blow up the world or the ultimate superman to rule it, and is set apart from the ordinary sane multitudes who go about their business innocuous and unsuspecting. Other cultures than our own might properly express their criticism of the sin of *curiositas* in this way; but our own culture is one in which *curiositas* has become a sin of the masses. All the innovations in medical technique which we have to discuss have been surrounded by a high level of publicity; none has been met with public anger, and one at least has encountered unaffected public satisfaction. The liberal revolution arose, and will continue to evolve, in answer to a mass desire of Western civilization, in which we all participate, and not at the behest of a few scientists. The pioneers of research give authentic expression to our society's soul, and we cannot be permitted to disown them.

The medical practitioner, then, finds himself an agent in the midst of a mass activity, and of course he can have no independence of action to speak of. If a certain medical technology has been developed, it is expected by society that he will facilitate his patients' access to it. To act in this sphere is to participate with the community's common action, which has very well defined and unnegotiable purposes. The paradox is that the community's goal is freedom; but such freedom clearly cannot include freedom of action which might frustrate communal action. It follows that we conceive our freedom passively, as a freedom not to suffer, not to be imposed upon. It is the freedom of consumers, rather than participants. It is a freedom to exist unmolested and unthreatened in the private realm, without interference in one's family, one's sexual relations, one's religion, one's eating and drinking — and, of course, the expression of one's opinion, for in a society in which politics is managed by technique, opinions are no longer potent in the public realm. The freedom of conscience on which liberal society prides itself is only a private freedom. As soon as one intends to act in public, by being a physician, a lawyer, or a journalist, one is constrained. To presume to exercise freedom of conscience in one's *public* dealings is, as we say, 'thrusting your private convictions down other people's throats', that is to say, bringing them out of the private realm into the public forum where they might challenge community policy. We call ourselves, self-deprecatingly, a 'consumer society', and chide ourselves for the greed which makes it so. Even the practice of medicine, it is often said, is seen increasingly as a kind of retail trade, marketing health-care to consumers. I do not think that this shift of perspective has primarily to do with an increase of greed or selfishness (though no doubt these are implied by it), but with our cultural conception of freedom as the freedom not to suffer. From such a conception it must follow that the freedom is all the patient's and the responsibility all the doctor's, and that is what evokes the analogy with the retail trades. The old conception of medicine as a collaborative enterprise, in which doctor and patient each have freedoms and responsibilities, can no longer be sustained.

All this, of course, has not come to pass without the encouragement of moralists. Modern moral philosophy is a diverse phenomenon; yet there are certain predominant features which mark the thinking of the last two centuries and which invite us to undertake the task of a general critique. (Alisdair MacIntyre's *After Virtue*[4] is a welcome sign that philosophers may now at last be ready to take up the invitation.) We could characterize these features in a number of ways: for example, in terms of its orientation to consequences or its preoccupation with the fact–value distinction. For the purpose of this discussion I am selecting only one which is especially relevant to medicine: the exclusive importance of compassion among the virtues.

[4] Duckworth, 1981.

Compassion is the virtue of being moved to action by the sight of suffering — that is to say, by the infringement of passive freedoms. It is a virtue that circumvents thought, since it prompts us immediately to action. It is a virtue that presupposes that an answer has already been found to the question 'What needs to be done?', a virtue of motivation rather than of reasoning. As such it is the appropriate virtue for a liberal revolution, which requires no independent thinking about the object of morality, only a very strong motivation to its practice.

Sometimes the philosophy of an age is epitomized in a work of art; and to my mind the modern programme for morality was never better expressed than at the very beginning of the modern period, in Beethoven's opera *Fidelio*, surely the greatest of all artistic tributes to the French Revolution. It appeared in 1805, fourteen years after Mozart's *The Magic Flute*; the difference between the two is the difference between two worlds. The journey from darkness to light which is charted in Mozart's masterpiece is presided over by the priest-king, Sarastro, who represents wisdom. In Beethoven's programme for enlightenment (I ascribe to him for convenience the ideas he found in the libretto by J. N. Bouilly) there is no place for a Sarastro, nor could there be. The story tells of a devoted wife, Leonora, who, in order to rescue her husband, Florestan, who has been imprisoned in the dungeons of the tyrant, Pizarro, disguises herself as a young man, Fidelio, and becomes an assistant to the jailer. At the point of crisis, when Pizarro is about to slay Florestan, she withstands him, and, as it were by a preordained fate, at that very moment the king's minister arrives to release the prisoners (all of them, it appears, political prisoners) and overthrow Pizarro's power. The message of the plot is simple: the revolution which will bring brotherhood in place of oppression is accomplished, not by the traditionally masculine virtue of wisdom, but by the traditionally feminine virtue of compassion, which must, however, clothe itself in the masculine attributes of 'Mut und Macht', resolution and might. When such an emotion assumes such a resolution, and is driven to say a decisive 'No' to tyranny, tyranny must fall before it. But how does it say 'No'? The crisis takes this form: Pizarro rushes at Florestan to strike him down with a *knife*, and Leonora–Fidelio interposes herself and stops the tyrant in his tracks with a *gun*. One can object that the moment is dramatically embarrassing: gun-powder is a *deus ex machina* for which the audience has not been properly prepared. But one would be wiser to think that it says exactly what Beethoven wished to say. Compassion, when it is driven to it, will arm itself with superior technique. Its strength over the enemy lies not, like Sarastro's, in its ability to appeal to nature, the way of wisdom, but in its ability to resort to artifice, the way of progress. In that moment on the stage the modern pro-gramme announced itself. Everything that we have to dis-cuss in these lectures was promised to us then.

We live not at the seedtime but at the harvest of the modern age, when we have the privilege of seeing what is its true character more clearly than those who have gone before us. And we have to think of the next seedtime, if one is given to us, and ask what we shall sow. In conclusion I wish to speak confessionally of how Christians should speak and think at this stock-taking point in our culture.

Christians should at this juncture confess their faith in the natural order as the good creation of God. To do this is to acknowledge that there are limits to the employment of technique and limits to the appropriateness of our 'making'. These limits will not be taught us by compassion, but only by the understanding of what God has made, and by a discovery that it is complete, whole and satisfying. We must learn again the original meaning of that great sym-bolic observance of Old Testament faith, the sabbath, on which we lay aside our making and acting and doing in order to celebrate the completeness and integrity of God's making and acting and doing, in the light of which we can dare to undertake another week of work. Technique, too, must have its sabbath rest.

Secondly, Christians should at this juncture confess their faith in the providence of God as the ruling power of history. To do this is to acknowledge that there are limits to man's responsibility with regard to the future, to deny that it can be an artifact which we can mould in its totality. This would be to recover the possibility of 'acting well', of contributing to the course of events a deed, which, whatever may become of it, is fashioned rightly in response to the reality which actually confronts the agent as he acts.

Thirdly, Christians should at this juncture confess their faith in the transcendent ground of human brotherhood. The equal partnership of one with another springs from a common standing before one heavenly Father. In our time the notion of brotherhood has broken up into two inadequate substitutes: on the one hand, the notion of bearing responsibility for someone, which implies care for the other's freedom without mutuality of action, and on the other the notion of association in a common project, which implies mutuality of action without care for the other's freedom. If we are to recover the mutual responsibility between doctor and patient, we need to think of their equality as co-operating human agents, in ways that only the Christian confession can open up to us.

Fourthly, Christians should at this juncture confess their faith in the Word which was from the beginning with God and without which nothing came to be, the Word which was made flesh for us in the person of Jesus. The understanding upon which we discern how to act, whether in medicine or in any other context, is not a matter of private conscience, nor of mass consensus. It is a public and publishable understanding that claims all mankind, whether or not it comprehends it. A Christianity which will bear witness to God's Word in Jesus will be a speaking, thinking, arguing, debating Christianity, which will not be afraid to engage in intellectual and philosophical contest with the prevailing dogmas of its day.

2. SEX BY ARTIFICE

We are asking about our human 'begetting', that is to say, our capacity to give existence to another human being, not by making him the end of a project of our will, but by imparting to him our own being, so that he is formed by what we are and not by what we intend. And we are asking what must become of our begetting in a revolutionary climate of thought in which 'making' is the conceptual matrix by which we understand all human activity. Given this general undertaking, the subject I address in this chapter may seem to be something of a diversion. For transsexual surgery has nothing to do with producing off-spring. Patients who undergo this surgical procedure can never subsequently be fertile, either in the sex into which they were born or in the sexual role which they have assumed. The whole enterprise of changing people's sex by surgery could appear to be a backwater, of little interest to those who have to wrestle with the problem of donated gametes and embryo manipulation. But with such a judge-ment I would have to disagree. I include the topic because I think it casts a great deal of light upon the characteristic patterns of thought which engage our attention when we have to discuss human fertilization. Let me first attempt a general explanation of how this is so.

In humankind natural reproduction is enabled by the differentiation of the sexes. It is because we stand over against one another, as men and women, as equal but complementary members of one human race, that we can, as a race, be fruitful. That is one of those connections that are given to us in the structure of human nature as we have received it — and received it, we must stress, not just from a particular culture or tradition, but from God. There is not, and never has been, any other humanity than the humanity which reproduces itself by means of the male-female relationship. Human parthenogenesis is a myth, in the most negative sense of the word; it is a fantasy in which we contemplate that which it is *not* given to us as human beings to be or do. If, in deference to an overarching evolutionary theory about the origin of species, we agree that the human race which reproduces itself in relationship emerged, by a long process of complexification, from beings which reproduced themselves in other ways, that is merely to say that the human was formed from the non-human. No being of this kind was ever part of the human race. If, on the other hand, we agree that in the conceivable future the development of cloning techniques may give the fantasy of human parthenogenesis an entrée into actuality, that will be a demonstration, if it occurs, that mankind does have the awesome technical power to exchange the humanity which God has given him for something else, to treat natural humanity itself as a raw material for contructing a form of life that is *not* natural humanity but is an artificial development *out of* humanity. The sheer difficulty of comprehending this staggering power which man can deploy may make us incline to minimize the significance of this, as of any other, technical innovation, projected or realized. The great intellectual challenge that faces our age in view of these innovations is not to understand *that* this or that may or may not be done, but to understand *what* it is that would be done, if it were to be done. And it would be mere intellectual evasiveness to pretend that the human mode of reproduction was a contingency that chanced upon our human race, and might as well not have done.

To this given connection in our nature between male-female relationship and procreation it is possible to respond in only two ways. We may welcome it, or we may resent it. Christian teaching has encouraged us to welcome it. Christian thinkers have said, in the first place, that the connection is good for the *man–woman relationship*, which is protected from debasement and loss of mutuality by the fact that it is fruitful for procreation. When erotic relationships between the sexes are conceived merely as relationships — with no further implications, no 'end' within the purposes of nature — then they lack the significance which they need if they are to be undertaken responsibly. They become simply a profound form of play, undertaken for the joy of the thing alone, and depending upon the mutual satisfaction which each partner affords the other for their continuing justification. The honouring of each partner by the other must be founded on the honour which the relationship itself claims, by serving a fundamental good of the human race. Saint Peter's counsel to Christian husbands (1 Pet. 3:7) has often been understood (rightly or wrongly) in this sense: 'Bestow honour on the woman, as you are joint heirs of the gift of life.' Paradoxically, this mutual honouring for the dignity of the procreative task can sometimes be seen most clearly in the midst of that mutual dishonouring which accompanies marital breakdown. When partners engage in a bitter struggle with each other over the custody of children, what does it mean but that even while they cannot bring themselves to live with each other, neither can they live without the image of the other gazing out at them through the child's eyes?

Christian teachers have said, in the second place, that the true character of *procreation* is secured by its belonging to the man–woman relationship. The status of the child as 'begotten, not made' is assured by the fact that she is not the primary object of attention in that embrace which gave her her being. In that embrace the primary object of attention to each partner is the other. The I–Thou predominates. The She (or He) which will spring from the I–Thou is always present as possibility, but never as project pure and simple. And precisely for that reason she cannot be demeaned to the status of artefact, a product of the will.

From these two complementary perspectives (the former more Catholic and the second more Protestant) Christian thinkers in the West have argued that the procreative and relational aspects of marriage strengthen one another, and that each is threatened by the loss of the other. This is a knot tied by God, which men should not untie. It is clear that any attempt to convert begetting into making constitutes a loosening of that knot, a severing of the relational from the procreative and the procreative from the relational. And for this to happen it is not necessary for anyone to deny the value of either procreation or sexual relationship. It is enough to think, as many moderns do seem to think, that each would flourish better if relieved of the burden of marching *pari passu* with the other. Not only would our offspring satisfy our natural reproductive and nurturing aspirations more fully if we could control the act of procreation more completely in its timing and its outcome; but our relationships would flourish more happily if they were relieved of what appears to be an unjustifiable burden of procreation. There are those who think (both conservative Roman Catholics on the one hand, and committed modernists on the other) that the modern programme of separating procreation from relationship was given and accepted by us *in toto* with the acceptance of contraception. I think this is both true and false. False, because the use of artificial contraception has never *necessarily* implied the modern programme, as certain other uses of technique necessarily do imply it — I shall argue this point further in chapter 5. True, because given the terms of the modern programme it was inevitable that contraception should be swept up into it and interpreted in the light of it.

In speaking of how transsexual surgery fits into this modern programme of thought, I want to guard against a possible misunderstanding. What I say is not intended to describe the motives which impel, or the reasons which persuade, either those patients who seek this surgery or the psychiatrists and surgeons who prepare them for it and perform it. I have no reason to suppose that patients are motivated by anything other than an urgent sense of need, and doctors by anything other than compassion. My remarks are intended to illuminate something rather different: the inexplicit programme of our liberal society in relation to sexuality, which has enabled it to accommodate such measures as these with comparative equanimity.

In the first place, the development of these surgical techniques encourages us to take the step in thought of conceiving sexual differentiation itself as artificial. (This may appear to be a rather bold implication to draw from a very limited technique which is practised on a very limited scale; I shall show presently that this thought does play an important part in one influential school of sexual theory, but it is enough for my present point that our culture is prepared, for its own a priori reasons, to *make* this leap of thought, whether or not it is really justified by the scope of transsexual surgery.) Once we think of it as possible to choose to belong to the opposite sex, once our sexual determination has become a matter of self-making, then, of course, even the vast majority who live, more or less comfortably, in the sex of their birth may be thought of as having chosen to do so. It is the standard temptation of a technological culture, as I argued in the last chapter, to conceive even the natural as a special case of artifice, to argue for letting nature take its course simply as the best of all instrumental means to some humanly chosen end. But the idea that sexual differentiation is dependent upon human will, necessarily brings into the sphere of the voluntary all that follows from it, including the possibility of procreation. That which depends on artifice is itself artificial. If it is a matter of choice that a man and a woman stand opposite one another as a 'natural' man and woman who can still beget children on each other's body, then that act of begetting is itself included in what has been chosen. Thus the general programme of artificializing procreation is furthered by the artificializing of sex.

In the second place, the artificializing of sexual differentiation helps to locate sexual relationships within the sphere of play. Artifice does not, of course, belong exclusively within the sphere of play; it belongs most importantly within the sphere of work. But device and ingenuity have a peculiar role in play. They flourish there freely and without constraint, not subject to the disciplines of utility. In play we do ridiculously clever things which serve no purpose, simply for the sake of doing them. Now, it would seem that there is an element of play that is entirely proper to erotic relationships. The element of spontaneity in sexual attraction, which has been so puzzling to some Christian theorists and which Saint Augustine attributed to original sin, is much better understood as marking the necessary link between love and playfulness. But the element of play is limited by the 'natural' ends of marriage, its ordering to procreation, to self-control, and to permanence. The more we detach erotic relationship from its natural ends, the more the element of play predominates, and with it the exploration of ingenuity and device within the erotic realm. It is not an accident, in other words, that a society which has sought to free erotic relationships from their procreative end, has also developed erotic fantasy and technique to a high level of sophistication.

Within this cultural setting the notion of someone's assuming a gender role opposite to that of his or her biological sex has an obvious location. It is, as it were, an extreme case of the liberal pursuit of unconstrained freedom in the private realm. Private existence (which is increasingly held to include all aspects of sexual existence, not only the erotic aspects) becomes a wide existential playground in which there is no objective reason for doing or being one thing rather than another, but in which one can exercise ingenuity for the sake of fuller self-exploration and self-disclosure. I repeat my warning: this is not intended as an account of what any transsexual patient, or any physician dealing with transsexual patients thinks or desires. It is an account of what we (that is to say, we in our liberal culture) think and desire, which makes us take this development in surgery very much in our stride.

Now let me turn from the social presuppositions and expectations which form the context for our discussion to the procedure itself and to the problems which it attempts to deal with.

The transsexual problem is, so far as has yet been established, a psychological problem only. A patient feels deep and continuing unease about his or her sex, and thinks that he or she should really belong to the opposite one. This feeling — 'gender dysphoria', as it is sometimes called in technical literature — is not necessarily lifelong, though it is clear that it does occur in children. It may alternatively emerge at puberty, in young adulthood or even in the mid-life crisis. It may, but need not, involve a quasi-factual conviction on the patient's part that he or she 'really is' a member of the opposite sex. More (biological) males are afflicted than females. It has proved more or less intractable to psychotherapeutic approaches. Most importantly, there is no apparent physiological abnormality. Thus the transsexual problem is prima facie quite distinct from the various types of physical sexual ambiguity often referred to generically under the name of 'hermaphroditism'. The attempt to relate transsexualism to hermaphroditism by the supposition of a hormonal influence is — so I am assured — a purely hypothetical one, for which there is as yet no experimental support. The implications of such an association for sexual theory would, of course, be very great.

There are now a large number of clinics throughout the Western world which deal with cases of gender dysphoria. They differ considerably both in standards of care and in philosophy. But among the more responsible a uniform type of practice is emerging, following standards of care prescribed by an international association based in San Francisco. Sufferers are coached extensively in assuming the appearance and actions of the sex to which they wish to belong, and in this they are assisted by hormonal treatment to control the secondary sexual characteristics. This phase is expected to have lasted for a considerable time and with complete success before a patient is eligible for surgical procedures. Selection for surgery is also dependent on wider considerations of general health. Then, in the course of a number of surgical operations, the patient's genitalia are reconstructed into a plausible replica of those of the assumed sex. Success is rather limited in the case of

the female-to-male patient, as the artificial male genitalia
are not capable of full sexual intercourse. Post-operative
patients continue to be heavily dependent on hormonal
treatment to the end of their lives in order to maintain the
appropriate secondary sexual characteristics. The principal
risk, which is obviously a very serious one, is that this
hormonal treatment may turn out to be injurious to a
health condition which develops later in life. A serious
heart condition, for example, or a neurological problem,
might confront the post operative transsexual with the
choice between death and the loss of the assumed sex-role,
which would imply a distressing reversion into a neither-
nor condition where the secondary characteristics of the
biological sex reappeared. It is a moot point, worth discussing in its own right, whether the awfulness of such a
misfortune constitutes a risk which ought to be taken, allowing for the distressing character of the initial condition
and its intractability to other approaches. But it is no part
of our concern to dwell on that question. I shall speak as
though the project of changing one's sex never went wrong,
and as though the techniques were perfected with respect
to female-to-male patients, and on that basis ask: what is it
that is being done, and why?

Two quite distinguishable answers are given to that
question by those who advocate and practise techniques of
transsexual surgery. One answer says that it *resolves an
ambiguity* of sexual differentiation in which the gender-
identity is discrepant with the biological elements of sexual
identity. Thus what is being done is analogous to what is
done when surgery is used to resolve a physiological ambiguity. The assumed sex is then taken to be the 'true' sex of
the patient in the only sense in which you can speak of a
'true' sex of someone whose sex is ambiguous, that is to
say, it is the sex in which it makes most sense for him or
her to live. The other answer is that the surgery *creates a
framework of pretence* with which the patient will find it
easier to live, and that this is done as a form not of cure
but of case-management. On this account it is not the

assumed sex but the biological sex which was the 'true' sex of the transsexual; the task of surgery has been to conceal that true sex in order to accommodate to the insuperable difficulties the patient experiences with it. In my booklet *Transsexualism and Christian Marriage*[1] I described these two theories, not wholly satisfactorily, as 'the psychological case' and 'the social case' respectively. I refer readers there for a more detailed account of them, and will be content at this point to discuss their implications in general terms.

1. The Psychological Case.

If we say of somebody with an unambiguous biological sex at birth — let us speak of a female-to-male transsexual: XX chromosome, with female gonads and genitalia perfectly congruent — that because her gender-identity does not accord with her body, she has therefore an *ambiguous* sex, we have made a major philosophical decision. We have collapsed the distinction between the physical sex and the psychological sex ('sex' and 'gender' in much common parlance). We have denied that the biological elements of her sexuality can comprise an unambiguous totality which can be set against, and contrasted with, her problematic psychology. Her sex is understood as an undifferentiated psychosomatic whole, a whole which displays ambiguities. From which it then follows that the process of her sex-gender development can no longer be understood as two processes — a physical sexual development, followed by a psychological development of gender — but only as a single undivided process which begins with the XX chromosome and ends in a consciousness, a consciousness in this case of unhappiness with her sex. But within this undifferentiated process social conditioning played a part. She was 'assigned' to the female sex at birth, and treated as a girl thereafter; and this helped to determine the development of her psychosexuality — unpredictably, as it happened. Now, if we respond to the ambiguous outcome of this total process

[1] Grove Books, 1982.

by surgically 'reassigning' her to the male sex, we are, apparently, not introducing any new influences upon the determination of her sex that were not already operative in the process anyway. Nature, nurture, and artifice have become indistinguishable elements in an undifferentiated process of necessity. This conception has been most consistently and determinedly argued by the American sexual theorist, John Money.

To the moral theologian the most interesting feature of this conception is that there is apparently no point at which human decision supervenes upon natural process. To speak of 'decision' and 'action' implies that we stand back from the world and respond to it, whether sympathetically or unsympathetically, by the self-determination of our wills. On this account, however, it appears that the surgeon never 'acts' in this sense, since the process of nature also embraces what he does; his technical intervention is simply the most mature and developed work of the natural process. Thus it might seem that we have to say exactly the opposite about this procedure conceived in this way to what we said about the general tendencies of technological society. Instead of treating nature as a special case of artifice, we treat artifice now as a special case of natural process.

But what a natural process! It is evident that the dominant factor in it is *society*. The most significant moments in the 'natural' process of sex-differentiation which begins with the XX chromosome and ends, now, with the construction of artificial male genitalia, are those in which society 'assigns' and 'reassigns' the patient, first to one sex and then to another. These are the only moments in the process that are conclusively determinative. Assuming as we must that gender dysphoria is a condition induced primarily by social influences, it appears, as we interpret this theory, that a malfunctioning social influence can be the decisive factor which vitiates a process that would be described as perfectly successful from a physiological point of view. If artifice is defended, then, as a manifestation of a *natural* process, this is only because the 'natural' process in question is in truth sociological. Society has become the supreme natural phenomenon. Beneath the surface of this theory the epistemological autonomy of the natural sciences has been undermined and replaced by a sociological epistemology, which gives priority in the interpretation of events to the social construction which is placed upon them. And this, I think, is a not untypical movement in modern thought. The natural sciences lose confidence in their ability to offer a description of natural reality in itself, and turn to the social sciences to make good the lack. But this turn to the social sciences constitutes an admission that reality-descriptions cannot be based on pure observation, but depend upon a construal that society will impose upon what is observed. And what is the meaning of this social construal other than the imposition of society's projects and purposes upon the way reality is understood — which is to say, the conversion of 'science' into 'technique'? It is manifestly clear how this is the case with the argument we are now considering. For it is our *will* to determine people's sex by assigning and reassigning them, which is used as proof that this is how people's sex is actually determined.

When a female child, assigned to the female sex at birth, grows up with a grave discomfort about being a member of the female sex, it is evidence, according to this theory, that for some reason or other our assignment of this person to this sex has not worked. The psychological problem of a cross-gender-identity is evidence for an incomplete work of nature (which is to say, of society). But the 'problem' is not that the patient has failed to come to terms with the reality of her female physiology, for we cannot speak of her female physiology as more 'real' than her male gender-identity which is the product of social forces. No, the problem is that there is a conflict between the status that society *conceives* itself to have conferred and the status that it has *actually* conferred. The problem is a clash between the perceptions which society has of this person and the perceptions which society (by some means or other) has given her to have of herself. Therefore the social construction of reality is at war with itself, and there is a resolution of the conflict to be made. A reconstruction of reality has to be undertaken around the feelings of the patient. Her (or 'his') feelings of resentment and dissatisfaction are the point at which society has to encounter the contradiction in what it has done. It has to take cognisance of these feelings if it is to bring its own function of sex-assignment to a harmonious and congruent conclusion. From the point of view of the patient, therefore, sexual self-definition is a project in which she has to struggle with society to exact a reality-concession. The writings of transsexual patients (who seem on the whole to belong to a literate and articulate section of the population) make it quite clear that this reality-concession is the real goal of their aspirations. Surgical reassignment, though desirable for itself, is valued more than anything because it represents society's acknowledgement that they are what they discern themselves to be. It is sometimes said that transsexual patients are 'manipulative', a charge which strikes me as intrinsically unjust. Since the whole undertaking is conceived on the basis that reality in sexual identity is conferred by social decision, it is hardly surprising that transsexual patients should do their utmost to extract reality-concessions from a society which announces itself to have made reality the way it is. We cannot blame the patients for playing by the rules society has laid down. One could perhaps regard transsexual surgery as a kind of grimly humorous *reductio ad absurdum* of sociological theories of reality.

2. The Social Case.

I will deal more briefly with the second type of theory, which I called 'the social case' in my booklet, though it has become clear that 'society' plays a dominant role in the first. It represents a kind of commonsense reaction against the extravagant reality-claims involved in the first. It is not inclined to acknowledge that people 'really are' the sex which they feel themselves to be, and takes an altogether more sceptical view of the struggle to dominate social perceptions of reality. This theory, when it speaks with scientific candour, is not prepared to say that someone with a healthy female body is suffering from a form of intersex ambiguity, but takes the view that she is a psychologically sick woman. It then proceeds to justify the hormonal and surgical treatment, not as any form of resolution but as a form of 'case-management', an effort to make life more liveable for the afflicted person by creating an environment of successful pretence within which he or she can live in comfort.

What, we may ask of this theory, is the nature of the concession that is being made to the patient, whom we teach to live and act like a man, whom we ask social institutions to accept as a man, and whose male role we finally reinforce by surgical operation? This policy for 'managing' gender dysphoria assumes, at the very least, a high degree of responsibility for relieving the patient of the burden of painful self-knowledge. Reinforcing the deviant gender-identity is reinforcing an illusory sense of how one relates to the world. What does it mean to live comfortably in the world on the basis of a pretence? And to what lengths should society go to reinforce a pretence in which someone feels comfortable? There is, it seems to me, a difference between saying, on the one hand, that when someone *does* exist comfortably on the basis of a pretence, one should not precipitately disrupt it, and saying on the other that society should marshal all its technological skill and social support-systems to buttress up a pretence that will always be fragile and vulnerable to the risk of such contingencies as heart-disease. The 'social case', though much more conservative than the psychological case in its reality-claims, has gone a lot further in the licence it has asserted for 'management'. It represents at its strongest the claim that political management (for it is essentially a *political* rationale that is here being offered) should relieve individ-

uals of the burden of tragic reality by taking responsibility
for dealing with reality out of their hands.

In the second place, and following from this, this theory
raises in a sharper form the question of the use of medicine
as an instrument of social management. For in conceding
that there is no *medical* rationale for this surgery (because
it attacks a healthy physiology in order to satisfy the demands of an unhealthy psychology) it overtly overrides the
traditional limitation of medical ethics that invasion into
the patient's body ought to be intended to do the body
good. Of course, transsexual surgery is certainly intended
to do the *patient* good; but it is not a *medical* good that it
is doing her, but a *social* good. And to serve that social
good, moreover, it adopts a procedure which is not even
medically neutral, but manifestly injurious. This justification of the procedure forces us to reflect upon the meaning of the old canon, *primum non nocere*. Has this not
always meant that an invasion into the patient's physical
constitution was to achieve physical and medical goods?
That the patient's body was not meant to be an instrument
which could be disposed of one way or the other to serve
some good that was not its own good? We cannot explore
at length the implications of the idea that surgery could
be used for the purpose of resolving social discrepancies
and inconveniences. It is enough to say that the fact of
the patient's voluntary co-operation in such a procedure,
though important, is not all-important. Not everything to
which people will consent, or which they will even demand,
is the right thing for *medicine* to undertake. For Western
medicine is premissed on a principle of Western Christian
culture, that bodily health is a good to be pursued and
valued for its own sake.

Let me in closing make an observation of a more confessionally Christian kind.

The sex into which we have been born (assuming that
it is physiologically unambiguous) is given to us to be
welcomed as a gift of God. The task of psychological
maturity — for it is a moral task, and not merely an event

which may or may not transpire — involves accepting this gift and learning to love it, even though we may have to acknowledge that it does not come to us without problems. Our task is to discern the possibilities for personal relationship which are given to us with this biological sex, and to seek to develop them in accordance with our individual vocations. Those for whom this task has been comparatively unproblematic (though I suppose that no human being alive has been without some sexual problems) are in no position to pronounce any judgement on those for whom accepting their sex has been a task so difficult that they have fled from it into denial. No one can say with any confidence what factors have made these pressures so severe. Nevertheless, we cannot and must not conceive of physical sexuality as a mere raw material with which we can construct a form of psychosexual self-expression which is determined only by the free impulse of our spirits. Responsibility in sexual development implies a responsibility to nature — to the ordered good of the bodily form which we have been given. And that implies that we must make the necessary distinction between the good of the bodily form as such and the various problems that it poses to us personally in our individual experience. This is a comment that applies not only to this very striking and unusually distressing problem, but to a whole range of other sexual problems too.

When God made mankind male and female, to exist alongside each other and for each other, he gave a form that human sexuality should take and a good to which it should aspire. None of us can, or should, regard our difficulties with that form, or with achieving that good, as the norm of what our sexuality is to be. None of us should see our sexuality as a mere *self*-expression, and forget that we can express ourselves sexually only because we participate in this generic form and aspire to this generic good. We do not have to make a sexual form, or posit a sexual good. We have to exist as well as we can within that sexual form, and in relation to that sexual good, which has been given to us

because it has been given to humankind. The service of
technique is appropriate and helpful within the limits of
that exercise.

3. PROCREATION BY DONOR

In this chapter I want to discuss the question of procreation with the aid of human gametes donated by a third party. It is a different sort of question from the other questions that I am discussing, in that we are not concerned here directly with the place of technical artifice in determining either sex or procreation — though, of course, the use of donated gametes arises only as a practical possibility because certain technical procedures have been perfected. The chief interest in this question, however, lies in the role of the third party *vis-à-vis* a marriage. It is to that question alone that I address myself in this chapter, postponing any direct observations on the *in vitro* techniques which have so extended the scope of donor procreation until Chapter 5. Until recently we have known of only one possibility for gamete donation, the so-called 'artificial insemination by donor', now several decades old. Today, however, we must talk not only of semen donation but of ovum donation, a possibility that has been created by *in vitro* technique. This, I shall argue, is by no means merely an equalization of the score between men and women, but a profoundly astonishing development. But I shall save my remarks on it until the end: the major part of this chapter will be given to matters which are common to ovum donation and semen donation. And in concentrating on the role of the third party, the donor, I shall not raise a number of issues that are rightly occupying the attention of the Warnock Committee and those who advise them, such as the dysgenic implications of undocumented donor fertilization, the selection of donors, and the commercialization of the practice through the buying and selling of gametes.

Let me begin with some observations on the purpose of gamete donation, observations which could be extended but must be made rather briefly and then returned to in Chapter 5. Its purpose, like that of other practices, is to overcome infertility, to allow a marriage to achieve the natural good which is set before human marriage in general, the good of procreation. As such its purpose is entirely in accord with the proper concerns of medicine: to overcome the sicknesses and failures in man's bodily nature which prevent natural goods from being realized. But this procedure, like others, does not overcome infertility by curing it, but by circumventing it. At the end of the day everybody is exactly as fertile or infertile as they were when they began. There is, however, a child. It is not a curative accomplishment, but a compensatory one. Does this make it improper? If we were to say so, we would be forced to take a very severe view of many established forms of medical assistance: prosthetic limbs, surgical boots, false teeth, all compensate for a lack which is caused by disease without actually aiming to cure the problem at its source. We can, however, say about these forms of assistance that they stand one step away from the central paradigm of medical practice, and that they do not lay claim on our sympathies with the same immediacy that the healing of disease does. They are things which it is good to do, and which it is good for medicine to be involved in doing; but they could not have an *overriding* claim to be done, comparable to the claim of those who are threatened by illness or injury to be healed and made well.

What distinguishes gamete-donation from other forms of compensation for infertility, *in vitro* fertilization with embryo replacement, for example, is the involvement of the third party, a personal representative, to take the place at a crucial point of one of the partners in begetting. The difficulty with personal representation in the begetting of a child, of course, is that begetting is an exclusively personal and private act. There are various tasks of life which an individual has to perform in the public realm, in which it is conceivable and necessary for him to be represented by others — in the vows of baptism, for example, or in any other legal or financial transaction to which he is a party while still a child. In medicine, consent to treatment is given on behalf of an unconscious or incompetent person by the next of kin. So the notion of acting for somebody in public dealings is not alien to us; but the more private the dealings, the more difficult it is to accept the notion of personal representation. What, for example, are we to think of marriage by proxy? The practice is not unheard of; but it is for the purpose of public ceremonial only. There is no nonsense about the proxy jumping into bed with the bride. How, then, can we even imagine personal representation in such a matter as begetting our children?

In the Old Testament there are two patterns of conduct which give us an inkling of how we might conceive of this difficult idea. One is the patriarchal pattern, in which the barren wife offers her maid to her husband as a substitute, for the purpose of bearing a legitimate child 'upon the knees', as it is said, of the wife, who would be deemed to 'have children through her' (Gen. 30: 3). This practice is recorded both of Abraham and of Jacob. The other pattern is given in the institution of levirate marriage, in which the widow of a dead man was to be married by his brother, with the intention that 'the first son whom she bears shall succeed to the name of his brother who is dead, that his name may not be blotted out of Israel' (Deut. 25: 6). We may observe in passing about both these patterns of representational begetting that they come from a social context in which the achievement of legitimate offspring was a matter of great importance for various social purposes, especially inheritance. We would fail to appreciate their significance if we did not see to what an extent the natural institution of marriage was borne down upon by the weight of social organization that rested upon the family unit. We are here very far from the typical modern case, in which a husband and a wife 'want' a child, for the sake of their own fulfilment and that of their marriage. However that may be — and I am far from denying that marriage in our own generation may suffer under comparable exigencies — what these examples suggest about the use of a representative in the act of begetting is that it depends upon a close relationship between the representative and the represented, so that there is some meaning in the transfer of responsibility. The patriarchal pattern depends upon the institution of slavery: Hagar, Sarah's maid, is at the disposal of Sarah. She is 'given' to Abraham by one who has the unquestionable right to do such a thing with her. The child she bears at Sarah's behest is delivered 'on Sarah's knees'. In the levirate pattern, on the other hand, the representative is the brother of the represented, on whom all the family responsibilities naturally devolve and who represents the dead members of his family simply by virtue of being who he is. From this point of view we must contrast the type of representation envisaged by both these ancient patterns with that envisaged by our modern practice of gamete-donation, in which the representative is deliberately anonymous.

The other thing we can learn from these Old Testament examples is to recognize a distinction between two kinds of representation. We may speak of 'representation by effacement' and 'representation by replacement'. In the patriarchal pattern the representative is subordinated to the one whom she represents. After the birth of Ishmael, as the narrative tells us, it was Hagar's refusal to accept subordination that, in effect, invalidated the representation. When Hagar 'looked with contempt upon her mistress', asserting herself as a mother in her own right against the mistress whose motherhood she was supposed to be assisting, the whole representational arrangement collapsed and the child Ishmael was disowned. By contrast, in the practice of levirate marriage the representative replaces the person whom he represents. Whereas Hagar, representing Sarah in her limited need, does not replace her but must continue as her dependent, the brother, who meets the infinite need of death, represents and replaces one who has otherwise disappeared from view. Only because he has disappeared can the representative replace him. Needless to say, this kind of replacing representation can be representation only on the public level. From the private point of view the brother has actually married his brother's widow himself; she is his wife, and the laws of their union are those of wife and husband, not of bride and proxy. Their children are his children. It is only for the public purposes of inheritance and succession that the first child can be regarded as the dead man's heir and not his own (cf. Ruth 4: 10, 13 for a comparable arrangement.)

The existing practice of AID, in which the donor, unknown and unrelated to any of the primary agents, steps in to provide his semen, and having done so effaces himself, vanishing without possibility of identification, recalls the first pattern of representation. The donor subordinates himself to the fatherhood of the husband by disappearing from sight. But there is a significant body of opinion calling for a reform of the practice, which would make it resemble more closely the alternative pattern, the pattern of representation by replacement. The model which attracts those who demand reform of this kind is that of adoption or step-parenthood. In adoption the social parents of the child act as parents to one who has been begotten by others. They take over the duties, responsibilities, and privileges of parenthood from those to whom they naturally belong, but who, by reason of death or simple incapacity, cannot assume them. They replace the natural parents where the natural parents have disappeared from the scene. Much contemporary opinion regards adoption both as a justifying analogy for the practice of AID and as a criterion for the reform of it. Particularly favoured among the proposed reforms is a qualification of the principle of donor-anonymity in the interests of allowing the child, when come of age, to establish his or her 'genetic identity'. Every AID child, it is suggested, should, shortly after the eighteenth birthday, have made available (should he or she wish to consult it) what is sometimes referred to as a 'genetic identity kit'. The interesting feature of these proposals is that many seem to envisage that the information will not be restricted to straightforwardly genetic matters — Is there a history of twinning in my genetic ancestry? Or of short sight? Or of males dying young from heart attacks? etc. etc. — but is supposed to include personal details — My father was a divorced ex-Irish stockbroker, a lapsed Catholic who played golf. The tendency of this is clearly to think of the donor as a *parent*, just as the adopted child has to learn to conceive of his natural parents as *also* his parents, as well as those whose child he has learned to think himself from the earliest days. The 'identity kit' thus becomes the means by which the vanished parent is still remembered in the world, and by which the child who is born to other parents remains, nevertheless, in one sense *his* child, just as the first son born to the widow and the brother became the heir of the dead man in the levirate practice.

But the more one considers the analogy with adoption, the more incongruous it seems to become. The natural parents of an adopted child have begotten the child. Their act, whether responsible or irresponsible, intended or unintended, has its own integrity and completeness. It is their act, and the child is unquestionably their child. This is the ground on which we think that an adopted child has the right to information about his biological parents. If, having given birth to their child, they disappear from the scene, it will be for others to represent them in the task of parenting; but that representation will, by serving the child that they have left, keep their name alive in the space which they have created for themselves and left empty. No such thing has been done by the donor of semen. He has not procreated; there is no space in the world which he has made for himself by his act, and which now needs to be filled because he is impeded from filling it. The act of procreation which takes place by artificial insemination is undoubtedly the act of the couple, and more particularly of the mother. It is not the donor's act.

We may be tempted to try to save the analogy by reversing it. Instead of seeing AID as a sophisticated form of adoption (conceived as 'replacement'), can we not, perhaps, see adoption as a primitive approach to AID (conceived as 'effacement')? In that case we would say, not that the biological parents are represented by the adoptive parents in their task of parenting; but that the adoptive parents are represented by the biological parents in their begetting. It is their need, the need for a child, that is met by the arrangement. But that leads us to even worse difficulties. The implication would be that the parents who begot a child did so *for the sake of* the parents who were to care for it. The biological parents acted in order to provide the adoptive parents with a child. The notion that adoption might be conceived in this way is very generally viewed with moral repugnance, and for good reasons. For whatever may be said about gametes, children are not property to be conveyed. The notion that one might undertake to become the parent of a child in order to alienate one's parental relation to another, implicitly converts the child from a person to a commodity. Notice that we do not have to introduce the notion of payment to make it repugnant. The suggestion of a commercial transaction merely underlines what is already present in the deliberate purpose of incurring a parental relation in order to alienate it.

That is why a good theory of adoption will insist, in the first place, that the biological parents will never cease to be the child's parents in a certain sense, and, in the second, that their replacement is occasioned only by their own incapacity to fulfil their role. They do not act for adoptive parents; adoptive parents act for them. It may be too easily forgotten, in an age when everybody's sympathies are claimed by the plight of couples who 'want' children and cannot have them, that in the act of adoption — however true it may be that it meets a 'want' in the adopting couple, however true it may be that they are richly satisfied by their love for the child — there is an element which can only be described adequately as charity — a coming to the aid of the natural parents, who have declared that they are unable to discharge their obligations to the child whom they have brought to life. It is at this point, it would seem to me, that the analogy between adoption and AID collapses completely. To take another's child into one's family is a totally different kind of act from taking another's gamete into one's act of procreation.

It is worth our while, however, to reflect on the reason that this analogy suggests itself and seems, though deceptively, to offer a way forward. It acknowledges the personal agency of the donor, instead of treating him merely as the purveyor of a useful material such as one might buy from a drug company. It acknowledges that, for the child at least, the personal identity of his genetic father cannot be a matter of indifference. It therefore implicitly acknowledges that the donor is, in a manner of speaking, personally present throughout the act of begetting. He is present in his genetic contribution, as a third party who will be the 'father' of the child. The current insistence on the significance for the child's self-knowledge of knowing at least what kind of person his or her father was, is unquestionably helpful, if only because it raises for us in its sharpest form the problem that lies at the root of gamete donation: how can the third party be personally present in the act of begetting, without being intrusive into the relationship from which the begetting springs? When some Christians insist that AID should be made available only to married couples, so that the child should have the benefit of a normal home life, are they demanding something self-contradictory? Is the personal presence of the donor not itself a disruptive factor in the marriage relationship, analogous to the personal presence of an adulterous lover or a rapist?

It seems to many that this offensive comparison is far-fetched, and that the question can be quickly dismissed. The donor has had no sexual intercourse with the opposite partner in the marriage. The sexual bond therefore remains unbreached by any alien personal presence, and we can speak, it would seem, without complication of a 'normal' married relationship which excludes third parties from the bond of affection, just as the marriage-bond is supposed to do. Should we accept this response as conclusive? I believe we should look both ways before we do so. For such a thesis forces the sharpest of dividing lines between the procreative and the relational goods of marriage. It invites us to think that if the relational good is fulfilled in an exclusive communion of sexual love, then the procreative good may be fulfilled in any way at all, not necessarily by an exclusive communion of procreational power.

It must follow from this, firstly, that the procreative good of marriage ceases to be the natural fulfilment of the relational good. As I argued in Chapter 2, when procreation is divorced from its context in man–woman relationship, it becomes a project of marriage rather than its intrinsic good; the means to procreation become the instrumental means chosen by the will, rather than themselves being of the goods of marriage. Correspondingly, sexual union itself is deprived of one of the features that give it its importance in human affairs. It can no longer be the case that the mingling of life in sexual union is a mingling that has both relational and procreative implications. It is no longer the case that the gift of self in sexual communion is at the same time a gift to the other of the possibility of parenthood. The divine blessing of children is no longer a blessing conferred *upon* this relational union of bodies with its promise of permanent affection and affinity. Children are now to be given (if the verb is still appropriate) by quite a different route. It would seem to me that those who insist that AID should be available only to married couples, do not value the *direct* contribution of sexual communion to procreation, but only the *indirect* contribution which it makes by establishing a secure and stable domestic context for a child to grow up in. That is what gives this insistence its slightly 'moralistic' flavour. It defends the link between married love and procreation only at the level of social order, while abandoning the underlying conception of that link as part of the ontology of marriage, the conception which originally made that form of social order seem necessary and right.

My argument, then, is that when we narrow our concern for the exclusiveness of marriage to the area of sexual

relations, leaving a wide-open field for third-party intervention in procreation, we have taken a fundamental and
decisive step towards 'making' our children. We have done
it by taking the procreative good of marriage away from
its natural root in the exclusive sexual bond of husband
and wife. That bond is allowed to go its own way, un-
encumbered by procreative implications, while we have
made a project of the will out of producing children. To
those who argue that this separation has been accepted in
principle when adoption has been accepted, I reply simply
that that is not the implication of the *best* understandings
of adoption. Adoption is not procreation, and does not
fulfil the procreative good of marriage. It is a charitable
vocation indicated to childless couples by the personal
tragedy of their deprivation in this area. And although it
may richly compensate for the sorrow and satisfy the
desire to nurture and educate children, it is still a substitute for procreation rather than a form of procreation.
This is not to belittle or demean the adoptive relationship.
Indeed, it might be said to praise it on altogether a higher
level, inasmuch as it points beyond the natural goods of
marriage to the supernatural good of charity. But adoption
cannot be taken as a precedent for interpreting procreation
as a simple enterprise of the will.

In the light of all this, we can form some idea of what
a Christian approach to gamete-donation must undertake
to show, if it wishes at once to justify its practice and to
appropriate the helpful insights which underlie the (otherwise misleading) analogy with adoption. If the gift of
semen is in some sense the gift of self, and if the donor is,
in some sense, personally present in the procreation and
can be called the father of the child, then the implications
of intrusiveness must somehow be offset. But that means
demonstrating a ground of community between donor and
husband, to make the alien personal presence less alien. We
need to restore the other element in the ancient practice of
representation by effacement, the element of belonging, so

that we can reasonably claim for the donor an identification with the husband's task of procreation.

In reading through a number of documents submitted by Christian bodies to the Warnock Committee, I was struck by one which seemed to understand very clearly what was required of a Christian justification for gamete donation. The Church of England Children's Society undertook to defend AID in principle (while advocating the usual reforms of its practice), but in doing so it found it necessary, as it said, to 'make explicit . . . the true nature of the contract'. Of the ten features of the AID contract which this document identified I single out five which appear to be central to the Society's argument: (i) the donation of sperm is given on trust that it will be used to further the gift of parenthood; (ii) the donation of sperm can never be to a mother, but is always to an intending father; (iii) the donation of sperm is a gift to compensate for male infertility, and therefore must be to a male; if sperm were administered directly to a woman with no male partner, the contract would be breached; (iv) the donation is absolutely anonymous, and the donor surrenders unconditionally all responsibilities for care and contact with the child; (v) wherever practicable the husband or male partner should be required to be present when the insemination is carried out, since it is being done on his behalf. The point of these proposals is clearly to bring the practice of AID under the discipline of a coherent concept of personal representation. The authors understand very well the difference beween AID and the kind of replacement-representation that forms the basis of adoption; therefore they insist strongly on the principle of anonymity. At the same time they support those reforms which would recognize the personality of the donor as significant. To overcome the problem of the depersonalizing implications of anonymity on the one hand, and the intrusiveness of the alien personality on the other, they develop a strong doctrine of male-to-male identification, through the notion of a contractual relationship between donor and husband.

Given this axis of collaboration, they seem to feel, the donor's personality is not intrusive (for he is there at the husband's behest) and his anonymity is not inhuman (for it arises out of sympathy for the husband and a wish not to stand in his way).

But no sooner have we appreciated the point which the authors of this document are trying to make, than we must doubt whether the purely contractual relationship they envisage can do the job they expect it to. So far as I can discern, they rely entirely on a shift in perspective to make this bond of identification between donor and husband a reality. It is true that they make one very valuable legal proposal, that ownership in genetic material should always be vested in the donor or the same-sex recipient, and never in a hospital or clinic. But in the last resort we must say that the male-to-male donative relationship of which they speak is a relationship on paper only, and does not establish any real ground of identification that can ease the problem of the alien presence. And what kind of identification, we must ask, might be appropriate for an act so personal? A friend may guide my hand upon the saw while I try to build a bookcase; but who may guide my hand while I embrace my wife?

In Old Testament society the representation of Sarah by Hagar worked (or was thought to work, though we need not suppose that the Biblical storytellers were much in favour of it) by virtue of the institution of slavery. Hagar had no property in her own procreative powers, which belonged prescriptively to her mistress. If we have doubts about the possibility of personal representation in the work of procreation, are our doubts not precisely the same doubts that we have about the institution of slavery itself — namely a repugnance at the thought that the personal powers of any human being, such as the power to beget children, could come to be regarded as the property of another? The identification of Hagar's procreative powers with the childbearing of her mistress implies their alienation from herself. The issue, as with slavery itself, is not primarily the issue of whether this alienation is voluntary or involuntary; it is whether it can happen at all, or be conceived to happen without a debasing and demeaning of the human person. We may perhaps still consider the other ground of personal identification which the Old Testament suggested to us. What if, taking a leaf out of the levirate marriage system, we suggested that the donor might be the husband's brother? Would we there have such a natural ground of identification between the two men that might make personal representation conceivable without intrusiveness and without the alienation of personal powers? And would this strong ground of identification compensate for the loss of anonymity, with the consequently limited possibility of self-effacement? I leave these questions as questions, not knowing how to answer them.

That suggestion aside, I must reach the conclusion that the only basis for a successful defence of gamete-donation is the outright denial that the donor is in any way personally present through his genetic contribution. We must regard the sperm and ovum rather in the same light as we would regard a donated kidney, as human material but not as personally human. Bodily spare parts are exchangeable because, although they belonged to someone in particular, and grew at the behest of his genetic constitution, they do not *convey* his genetic individuality. We will have to treat gametes as though they were interchangeable in the same way. This would mean, in effect, that we resolved to continue with AID in exactly the same form as it is now practised: we would be indifferent to the identity of donors, we would dismiss suggestions for genetic identity kits, we would have no serious objections to the payment of donors for their services, we would regard the social father of the child as for all conceivable purposes the real father. We would, in fact, deny that the 'personal' element in begetting had anything to do with genetic inheritance.

And if we cannot do that? If we cannot achieve either the pre-scientific innocence or the post-scientific hardness of heart which is necessary to ignore the presence of the

personal in the genetic? If we still find ourselves thinking
of the gift of sperm or ovum as a gift of self, and if we still
revolt against the idea that it might be saleable? If we still
think of the donor as in some way the parent of the child,
and the link between him and the child something that it
may be necessary for the child's sense of identity to have
explored? Then, it seems to me, we should recognize that
we are thinking in terms which, of themselves, ought to
make AID unthinkable. We are thinking in terms of a third
personal presence in procreation, a presence which cannot
be effaced.

All these considerations, which we have worked through
largely in relation to the established practice of AID, will
also apply to the not yet common practice of ovum
donation. I must, in conclusion, point in a sketchy and
unsatisfactory way to the new issues which are raised by
the new practice — if only to raise an eyebrow in public
about the very common assumption that there are no new
issues, but only those already familiar to us from the AID
discussion. I quote an exchange between Doctor Johnston
and Doctor Fishel, from a discussion at the Bourne Hall
conference of 1981:[1] 'Johnston: If AID is acceptable then
oocyte donation should be equally acceptable. All it involves is the transfer of one of two gametes to help an
infertile couple . . . Fishel: There is one difference between
sperm and oocyte donation. With a donor oocyte, the
woman is not carrying her own child . . . . Johnston: This
is a fine legal point.' For the first time in the history of
humanity a woman is pregnant with a child which she did
not engender. For the first time in the history of humanity
children are born with three biological parents, two genetic,
one physiological. It may be that some of those who have
followed me patiently so far have begun to suspect that
my opposition of 'begetting' and 'making' has a savour of

[1] R. G. Edwards and J. Purdy (eds), *Human Conception in Vitro* (Academic Press, 1982), p. 359.

the rhetorical about it. Am I making an extravagant meal out of small developments which really amount to nothing? If I have to defend myself against that charge, I will simply remind you that there are a few human beings alive today who have three biological parents. If talk of 'making' our progeny fails in any way, it fails only by falling short of this unplumbed chasm that has opened up in our experience of what it is to be human, a work of technique before which understanding is numb. I am reminded of Hannah Arendt's telling remark about the atomic scientists who developed the earliest nuclear weapons: 'They move in a world where speech has lost its power.' It is because we can neither think nor say what it is that we have done, that we are forced to hide our gaze from this quantum leap in human reality, and describe it as a 'fine legal point'.

What *in vitro* techniques have apparently done is to divide the female role in procreation into two: the contribution of the ovum and the pregnancy. We may therefore assign the action of begetting to three *personae dramatis* instead of two. The question now arises: on the assumption that we still expect to retain the conventional pattern of social parenthood, that is, a family of two parents of opposite sex, to which two persons does the parental role really belong? We have a major problem of parental ownership. (I shall use the phrase 'parental ownership' as the most economical way of expressing that 'belonging' which is the proper relation of a child to its parents, and ask you to rid your minds of any distracting connotations of disposable property which our more common talk of 'ownership' may suggest to you.) The problem of parental ownership was, of course, already present in germ in the AID discussion, when we had to decide whether the donor was or was not the 'father' of the child. But it appears in quite new dimensions when we begin to deal with three biological parents.

The implications of AID, as *presently* established, would seem to be clear. Genetic parenthood is not relevant to the question of parental ownership. The parental role belongs to the mother who bears the child and derivatively to her spouse. Genetic parenthood is not parenthood in its fundamental sense. Gamete donation is possible precisely in order to enable *another* person to become a parent. The husband's parenthood is ensured by his social and sexual relation to his wife, whose own parenthood is given in the fact of her pregnancy — for although she can also claim genetic parenthood, the displacement of the donor makes it clear that genetic parenthood does not matter. On this understanding, then, the practice often described as 'womb-leasing' or 'surrogate motherhood' must be deemed conceptually impossible. The child belongs to the womb that bore it, irrespective of who the genetic parents are. Any contractual arrangement concerning the return of the child to the genetic parents after birth could only be understood as a contract to *adopt* the child.

But that is on the basis of AID as now practised. As we have seen, current practice is under question, and genetic parenthood is in some quarters thought to be more important than current practice would allow. We might therefore be tempted in the opposite direction, to say that genetic parenthood is what really counts. In that case womb-leasing becomes a possible conception, but gamete donation has to be reinterpreted, in ways that we have already traced, as a form of adoption. If we are to find a middle way between these two, it will be hard to avoid coming down with some arithmetical proposal. We might say that parental ownership would reside in any couple who, being married or deemed married at the time of the child's conception, contributed between them two out of the three elements necessary to the procreation of a child: either two gametes, or one gamete and the pregnancy. This would allow AID (the wife contributing both the ovum and the pregnancy) and womb-leasing (the husband and the wife each contributing their genetic inheritance). It would not allow us to conceive of the combination of ovum donation and womb-leasing, since the donor, by contributing two elements out of the three, would thereby become the parent of the child.

It would give us no way of resolving parental ownership in certain cases of double gamete-donation, when the child was born to a woman who had not contributed the ovum herself and the semen came from a man who was the partner of neither of the women.

These speculative suggestions sound grotesque in our ears, and our humanity shrinks from considering them seriously. Yet the tragic situation is that unless some rule of this kind is adopted, we shall be left with an inevitable and highly distressing outcome. Parental ownership will be determined simply on the basis of contract. The same practices will then yield different results for parental ownership depending on the terms of the contract in each case. 'Womb-leasing' is the same in practice as one form of double gamete-donation; only the contractual arrangements for assigning parental ownership will distinguish them. AID is the same as the combination of ovum donation and womb leasing. In this worst of all worlds, to which we shall unhappily come fast, unless the Warnock Committee, and its equivalents in other Western states, grasps the nettle with great firmness, the last shreds of a connection between procreation and being will be torn asunder. Humanity will be made under contract, with all the component parts legally conveyable. There will then be no reason to insist that parental ownership should reside in a person who had any physical stake in the child at all. One could conceive of a couple arranging to have a child put together, choosing the three contributors they thought most competent for the work.

From this dismal prospect we may well shrink, and pray (as I suspect we are often tempted to do in the face of scientific 'inevitabilities') that by the time we get there we may have lost the humane sensibilities which make us so distressed to contemplate them now. The process I describe has at least this much inevitability about it. Where natural constraints are removed, more is left open to human decision; and in a liberal society, failing exceptional public concern, that decision, especially in this kind of area, will

probably be left in private hands, which means, to individual contractual arrangements. What is distressing to us
about this outcome is the seeming arbitrariness of it. But
of course it would be equally arbitrary for the government
simply to lay down a rule — say the two-parts-out-of-three
rule which I suggested just now. Arbitrariness is what we
have wished upon ourselves. In the natural order we were
given to know what a parent was. The bond of natural
necessity which tied sexual union to engendering children,
engendering to pregnancy, pregnancy to a relationship
with the child, gave us the foundation of our *knowledge*
of human relationships in this area. Now that we have
successfully attacked the bond of necessity (and artificial
insemination was the first blow struck against it), we have
destroyed the ground of our knowledge of the humane.
From now on there is no knowing what a parent is.

4. AND WHO IS A PERSON?

When experimental procedures are carried out upon hu-man subjects for whose individual treatment they are not designed, then, according to the Declaration of Helsinki, the subject must be a fully consenting volunteer, and the investigator must discontinue research if at any point it appears to be harmful to the subject. The position of children and of other patients incapable of giving informal consent is ambiguous, but certainly protected. A strict view maintains that they cannot properly become the subjects of such research at all, because parents or guardians could not give valid consent to any procedure which offered them no benefits and involved the risk of harm. If this strict view is not followed, they are, nevertheless, still protected, both by their guardians' right to withdraw consent and by the principle that research must be discontinued if it appears to be likely to become harmful. By these restraints (which can constitute a grave inconvenience to research) we acknowledge that the 'human subject' is in fact a 'person', not simply to be imposed upon, for whatever good or socially useful end, nor to be directly harmed, however great the indirect harm that may accrue to others.

Our subject in this chapter is experimentation on human embryos, to which none of these restraints apply. But in order to get a good view of this practice we need to explore what is meant by the term 'person'. For in conducting ex-periments upon early human embryos, experiments which comprise the full extent of their short existences, begin-ning with fertilization *in vitro* and ending with discard and death, we say as unambiguously as we can that they are not 'persons', that they are disposable to the ends of society, and that harm may be done to them for others' good.

The concept of 'person', though with a background in the classical world, first assumes major theoretical import-ance for the understanding of human existence with the

Christian writers of the early centuries of our era. It is not a biblical term (unless we are to take note of the rather unencouraging comment of Saint Peter that God is 'no respecter of persons' (Acts 10: 34)), but it gains its hold on Christian thought as the early Fathers attempt to state with precision, not indeed what the Christian faith holds about man as such, but what it holds about the tri-personal God and about Jesus Christ, both God and man and yet one person. It was these high themes that made them dissatisfied with the conventional classical ways of conceiving agency and individuality. It is true that the term 'person' does not become part of a theological doctrine of *man* until the very end of the patristic period, with Boethius. But the concept always had implications for the Christian understanding of man, and it is evident how the Fathers, even while they still used classical vocabulary, were shaping their view of man in accordance with it, which is really simply to say, in accord with the Biblical ways of understanding individuality.

When we speak of a 'person', we speak of a *persona* — and it is well known that that term had special associations with the ancient theatre, where the *persona* was the character-mask. We speak, therefore, of an *appearance*. It is the appearance of an individual human being; the Greek equivalent means, simply, 'face'. But in invoking the theatre we also invoke the thought that what is presented there is not a tableau, but a story. The *personae dramatis* are not mere faces, but characters who have their exists and their entrances, whose appearances and reappearances constitute the drama. In the ancient theatre one actor might often play more than one part, and one part might be split between two actors. The intelligibility of the drama, therefore, depended on the continuity of the mask, so that the spectators would recognize, not simply the reappearance of the actor but the reappearance of the character. A *persona* is an individual appearance that has continuity through a story. It is the appearance of an agent to whom things happen and who does things, of one who has, as we say, a 'history'.

If we look at a herd of cattle in a field, we can pick out individual cows from the mass. But no cow has a 'history' in the sense that an individual human being does. Which is to say that although cattle, like human beings, live individuated lives which are extended through time, there is no particular significance which resides in the individual life-course of each. It does not constitute a 'story'. When Abraham entertained the three heavenly visitors by his tent at Mamre, he slaughtered a calf. Has anyone ever asked *which* calf? Yet you could not slaughter a human being without slaughtering some particular human being, someone with a name, of whom it would make sense to ask 'Who was it that died?' Even if you slaughter hundreds of thousands of human beings at one blow with a strategic nuclear weapon, people whose names you will never know and whose faces you will never have seen, it will still be the case that they *had* names and stories, that the history of some Dmitri or some Anna has been brought suddenly and irreplaceably to an end, and that that *unique* event has happened hundreds of thousands of times in one moment. Individual humanity does not lose its significance when it is part of a multitude; rather, the history of the multitude gains its significance from the fact that it is a multitude of persons, not of ants, each of whom has a significant history in him- or herself.

To speak of a 'person', then, is to speak of 'identity', that which constitutes sameness between one appearance and another, and so makes us beings with histories and names. It was inevitable that this category should appear more satisfactory to Christian thinkers than the purely *qualitative* categories with which ancient classical philosophy had undertaken to analyse man — such categories as 'intellect', 'soul' etc., which had no historical dimension. For they found in the Old and New Testaments the thought that the identity of human beings had to do with their role in history, a role that was assigned them by divine providence. And this was not only true of the prophets, of whom it could be said 'Before you were in the womb I knew you, and appointed you a prophet . . .' (Jer. 1: 5). It

could be said also of wicked Pharaoh, 'For this purpose
have I raised you up . . .' (Ex. 9: 16), and even of indifferent Cyrus, 'For the sake of my servant Jacob I call you
by your name' (Is. 45: 4). And to move altogether out of
the realm of world-historical figures into the daily life of
humble people, such a practice as we considered in Chapter
3, the practice of levirate marriage, is only one of many in-
dications in the Old Testament of how identity in ancient
Israel was tied up with inheritance — not in the conservative
sense in which we might say with Anthony Trollope that
it is 'certainly of service to a man to know who were his
grandfathers', but in a forward-looking way, in which someone would achieve significance by having grandchildren,
and so contributing to the history which God destined for
his people with all its families and tribes. Which is not to
say that a person's identity is *exhausted* by the history of
which she is part, so that we are not speaking in the end
of a subject at all but only of a sequence of events; but
simply that her identity is *historical*, that is, it makes a
sequence of events *into someone's history*.

In the light of this we can understand how patristic
Christian thought, developing as it did in two main
languages, Latin and Greek, was able to use interchange-
ably two words which had different nuances. The Latin-
speaking church spoke of a *persona*, a term with its associations in the theatre and the law-courts, which suggested
that the person was an 'agent', one who could appear, or
hold a part, in the public realm. The Greek-speaking church
came, more slowly, to speak of a *hypostasis* (literally, a
sub-stance), which suggests a reality which *underlies* or
supports all the characteristics and qualities, all the variable
appearances which one and the same person might present.
We might most helpfully render *hypostasis* as 'subject'.
The difference of emphasis in these two terms caused problems of mutual understanding, but the common element
was the emphasis on continuity and historicity. When one
spoke of a 'person' one spoke of these different, success-
ive, and changing appearances as one connected appear-

ance; when one spoke of 'hypostasis' one spoke of something that underlay them all and so made them one, the hidden thread of individual existence on which, so to speak, they were all hung like clothes on a line. The identification of *hypostasis* with the concept of 'substance' undoubtedly causes confusion in the modern philosophical context, where the categories of substance and history are frequently opposed. But that opposition is not relevant to our exposition, for classical Christian thought never contemplated the supposition of modern thought that one's history is something that one makes *for oneself*, one's identity something that one determines *for oneself*. In the Old and New Testaments Christian thinkers found a different kind of historicity that must be attributed to the individual human being, a historicity given to him, not as a mere open-endedness in temporal existence but as a definite vocation from God which constituted him as a person, a 'someone who ...' this that or the other, from before his first act or thought.

The concept of 'person', then, in both its Latin and its Greek form, was set in opposition to a *qualitative* analysis of what it is that gives us our identity. The ancient world could comfortably say that our identity resides in the *soul*; but the early Fathers quickly saw that if they were to think of the divine–human identity of Christ in such terms, they would either have to deny him a human soul (and so deny him some human qualities) or, in attributing to him a human soul, would have to attribute to him a purely human identity. Apollinaris in the fourth century proposed that the church should think of Christ's identity, and so of all human identity, as self-conscious, action-directing *mind*; and that it should say that in Jesus the human mind was 'replaced', as it were, by the Divine Mind. But the church found that it could not say that Jesus lacked a human mind — for that, too, would be to deny him certain human qualities. By way of these false starts, the Christian thinkers of the patristic age learned that no qualitative term would ever do to express Christ's individual identity, and so (by implication) that no simply qualitative term would ever do to express identity as such.

The landmark which most conveniently shows how lessons learned from the debate about Christ were appropriated for human identity in general is the famous definition of Boethius' Fifth Tractate, with which every philosophical article on the concept of 'person' begins. A person is 'the individual substance of rational nature'. For Boethius, defending the Chalcedonian definition of Christ as 'one person in two natures', it was paramount that the concepts of person and nature should be kept distinct. A person is a substance, and a nature is the 'specific property' of a substance; it is not the case (as supposed by heretics on all sides) that to every nature there corresponds a person. In other words, the distinctive qualities of humanity are attributable to persons, not persons to the qualities of humanity. Yet there are ambiguities left unresolved. It is still a criterion for personhood that its nature should be 'rational'. When Boethius' substantialist understanding (or his Aristotelian presentation of it) was eroded, and his Christological basis forgotten, it became possible to read his words in another way, as though a person were merely the *particular instance* of a rational nature. The history of the concept 'person' is the history of how 'nature' takes over from 'substance', the secondary feature of the definition displacing the primary one.

Once Christian thought modified qualitative conceptions in favour of substantial–historical conceptions, it was committed to asking certain further questions about identity. When does it begin? and when does it end? These questions, which are by no means either obvious or necessary questions to ask about purely qualitative categories (such as 'soul' or 'mind') become both obvious and necessary as soon as identity is conceived in a historical way. A number of classical writers wrote treatises entitled 'On the soul' (*Peri psuchēs*, or *De anima*), but it took a Christian thinker, Augustine of Hippo, to entitle a treatise of philosophical anthropology 'On the soul's beginnings' (*De origine animae*).

The question 'When does the person begin and end?' is a question about the meaning of birth and death. Could anyone actually *avoid* this question who was at all attentive to the contents of the Bible? The ancient world could indeed push this question to the edges of its concern — still not completely avoiding it, for there are, of course, famous ancient speculations both about the pre-existence and the immortality of the soul. Yet it could go a long way simply by treating birth and death as the outer parameters of personal identity. But the immediate implication of the Gospel of Jesus' resurrection, as Saint Paul well understood when he wrote 1 Corinthians 15, is to demand that this marginal question should immediately be brought to the centre, at least as far as concerns personal identity in the face of death.

With regard to birth the implications are less immediate. Yet it would be quite mistaken to suppose that in assembling stories about the conception and birth of John the Baptist and Jesus, Saint Luke was merely adding a decorative motif to a Gospel that could very well have done without them. In Jesus' birth there is a new beginning — in his birth, not only in his first preaching mission. It is a decisive new beginning, but not unforeshadowed. It fulfils prophetic hopes of previous ages for a new beginning, hopes which could find provisional expression even in *other* births than that of the one conceived of the Holy Spirit of the Virgin. So Saint Matthew can refer us back to Isaiah the prophet's word to King Ahaz that, in the tormented international politics of the eighth century BC, his hope lay in the sign that 'a young maid shall conceive and bear a son and shall call his name Immanuel'. Presumably there was an Immanuel born in the eighth century; his politically significant birth anticipated and foreshadowed for the evangelist that much more significant birth of the later Immanuel. And then there is the great interest that Saint Luke shows in John the Baptist's conception and birth. For even in the birth of others, besides the Messiah himself, the new beginning which God purposes can be discerned, and in the giving of the name, 'Immanuel' or 'John', believing parents declare their faith in the story which, under God's direction, is about to unfold. Above all in the gift of a child to the barren (where nature itself has refused to give a child) we see the intervention of God to make a new start, to create a 'history' — which nature alone can never do.

These theological observations do not of themselves yield any very precise view of the beginnings of individual identity. What they do, however, is to keep that question at the centre of our Christian thought about man, and forbid us to relegate it to the periphery. For more precision (which is necessary for us as it was not necessary for Saint Luke) we must learn from what scientists can tell us about where the story of each individual begins. Previous generations of Christians, making the best use of such empirical observations as were available to them, formulated the theory of a point of 'animation' some time after conception. Our own generation has fuller empirical knowledge, which seems to suggest a different answer. Geneticists tell us that in the fusion of sperm and ovum a new genome is formed which controls subsequent personal development, in so far as that development is genetically controlled in principle and not affected by environmental contingencies in practice. This observation seems to provide an indication of the beginning of a new personal history at conception.

That last awkward sentence is, in fact, rather carefully phrased. It means no more and no less than what it says. No more — for in the first place, genetic *discontinuity* does not of itself indicate individual personal identity. Parental gametes, we are told, are also genetically distinct from the genetic constitutions of the parents. The point is simply that the personal identity of conceptus with child is indicated by the genetic continuity which makes one become the other. In the second place, genetics can only indicate, and cannot demonstrate, personal identity. 'Person' is not a genetic or a biological category; to observe a gene is not to observe a person. What genetics can do is to show us an *appearance* of a human being which has decisive continuities with late appearances. It remains for another mode of knowledge to discern the hypostasis behind the appearances. In the third place, we can only say provisionally that the science of genetics *seems* to provide such an indication. We cannot overlook the possibility either that geneticists may change their minds about how to interpret what they have seen, or that other investigators may yet describe discontinuities between conceptus and child which may, in the event, appear more fundamental. I take it that the argument from foetal wastage, much favoured by those who dispute the conclusiveness of genetic testimony in this discussion, is meant to draw attention to just such a discontinuity. My reservation about it is that I do not see how a merely *statistical* argument can give us a sufficient indication of discontinuity in *individual identity*. There seems to be a category-leap, which can only be defended on the thesis that nature is perfect and never wastes human beings — a hypothesis that is manifestly false. The most that the argument can do, it would seem to me, is to provide corroborative support for an alternative description of human beginnings which had independent force.

Against these three qualifications to the use of genetic testimony there is still to be set the 'No less'. We cannot ignore the fact that such science as we have today speaks to us of this point of new beginning at conception. Anyone who is dissatisfied with the conclusiveness of this science might properly do as Roman Catholic thought does — declare ignorance about the beginnings of personal existence and then protect the child from conception on a play-safe basis. Anyone, on the other hand, who is going to be wiser than this science, ought to offer an alternative account which will be sufficiently conclusive to render the appeal to genetics irrelevant. It seems to me (if I may venture a generalization about the contemporary debate) that the most favoured alternative account, which relates personal identity to brain-function, is inconclusive because it rests on a *philosophical* preference rather than a scientific one, a preference for *qualitative* conceptions of personal identity such as the early Christian thinkers confronted and found wanting.

Perhaps the simplest way of characterizing the modern preference for qualitative conceptions is to refer to Immanuel Kant's famous 'practical imperative': 'Act so that you treat humanity, whether in your own person or in that of another, always as an end and never as a means only.' In exploring the implications of this Kant argued that what is valuable in humanity is 'rational nature' (a revenant from Boethius' definition), which must always respect itself — 'whether in your own person or in that of another'. Notice the phrase '*in* your own person'. A person is here an individual being *in whom* a generic principal of rational nature is discerned. What evokes our esteem, what forms the 'objective end' of our moral law, is the generic 'rational nature' rather than the individual in which it makes its appearance. This constrasts neatly with the Chalcedonian definition of the person of Christ, in which he is said to be 'one person *in* two natures': the person, the individual being, is primary, and is discerned in the two complementary complexes of attributes, the human and divine natures, which he possesses.

Characterisitic also of the modern conception is the use of the abstract noun 'personality'. It is, as it sounds, a qualitative term. It suggests certain attributes which will not only be possessed by individuals whom we encounter as persons, but will constitute what it is to be 'personal'. We say of a beautiful being that it is something which possesses beauty. Why not say also of a personal being that it is something which possesses personality? When a modern thinker proceeds in this way he invites us to agree that what we have to look for is something qualitative, something that an individual being may or may not turn out to possess, a complex of capacities, abilities, possibilities, performances, associated, perhaps, with 'rational nature', which will be recognizably 'personal'. Now, we need not deny that there may be such a complex of attributes which does generally characterize persons, and which we may, without offence, call 'personality'. But that complex is not what Christians have meant in the past when they have referred to 'persons'. It ignores the other aspect in Boethius' definition, the 'individual substance . . .', which does not point to a quality, or complex of qualities, but to a 'someone who . . .'. To a person in *that* sense these qualities may belong, but he is not one with them; he acquired them as events in his history.

Now at last we begin to have our summit in view. For the modern qualitative conception of the person as individuated personality will tend to encourage two further projects of thought. First, it will encourage us to bring personality under the observation of experimental knowledge; secondly, it will encourage the differentiation of personal from pre-personal human existence. And it seems to me that from these two adventures of thought, experimentation on human embryos must be a natural, one might almost say a necessary, outcome.

We may decide whether or not any being manifests 'personality' by testing for it. There are many ways in which this complex of attributes, capabilities, and performances may be proven experimentally, from the simplest behavioural test (speaking, and seeing whether one is answered) to the most sophisticated biological test. But we cannot decide in this way whether or not any being is a *person*. We discern persons only by love, by discovering through interaction and commitment that this human being is irreplaceable. Perhaps we only discover this, in the fullest sense, of a few human beings in the course of our lives, though we would have inklings of it with many more. If we assert that it is true of all human beings, we do so by a kind of faith (not unrelated to Christian faith) that the significance we have discerned in those we have loved is a significance which God attributes to all members of Adam's race. It is possible to refuse this act of faith; it is never provable in a demonstrative sense. Yet without it we would lack any ground for committing ourselves in personal relationship to those whose 'personality' we could not discern — to children in the womb, for example, or to the severely handicapped. If in the end we come to discern that these too are persons, irreplaceable and irreducibly important, we do so only after, and not before, we have committed ourselves to them in personal interaction. 'Who is my neighbour?' asked the lawyer of Jesus. 'Who', Jesus asked in reply, 'proved neighbour to the man who fell among thieves?' To discern my neighbour I have first to 'prove' neighbour to him. To perceive a brother or a sister, I have first to act in a brotherly way. To know a person, I have first to accept him as such in personal interaction. Quite different from this is all experimental knowledge, which is acquired by achieving a masterful *distance* on its object in testing and proof. Such knowledge cannot be knowledge of the hidden, of that which underlies appearances. It looks for appearances and it finds appearances. Its scope is limited to that which it values in the first place, the publishable 'qualities' of rational nature or personality.

Given this limitation to his scope of interest, the modern thinker will be forced to make distinctions between human appearances which do, and human appearances which do not, manifest the qualities which he values. How he makes this distinction will vary considerably, depending in part on whether he has a conservative or a revolutionary temperament. Will he, for example, include severely brain-damaged patients in the class of the personal or of the impersonal? But some attempt at distinction appears unavoidable to him. From this arises the modern preoccupation (popular among conservative moderns) with the presence of brain-function in the early foetus. Here is a testable level of functional capacity without which the attributes of personality cannot be projected. There are, of course, other necessary conditions for personality; but brain-function suggests itself because of our tendency to see the brain as the point at which rational and spiritual possibilities are rooted in man's physical constitution. Unless our modern thinker is a very crass materialist (which few are, even among those who would like to be) he will not simply set an equation sign between the brain-function and personality, but will conceive personality as a complex of qualities which arise out of the functioning of the brain. Brain-function thus appears to him to be a safe lower limit for the purposes of practical decision. In its absence he can speak confidently of the absence of personality, though he is not committed to thinking that personality is even vestigially present wherever a minimal brain-function is established.

Here, then, we have the two constituent elements of which our practical attitude to human embryos will be composed: on the one hand, a conviction that human personality can be the object of experimental knowledge; on the other, a conviction that humanity can be divided into the personal and the non-personal, which is to say for our purposes the pre-personal. Yet in order to understand how these two elements form the basis of an imperative necessity to conduct experiments on embryos, we need to recall from previous lectures a third factor: the devotion of our society to the enhancement of personal freedoms. In a liberal society it is the private activities of life — love-making, begetting children, eating and drinking, making a home, and exchanging opinions and views — that are thought to be the true home of personality; and the goal of our liberal revolution is to free them from the constraints of government, religion, and natural necessity. This is bound to lead to a concentration of thought and experiment on human biology was somehow *wrong*, though popular ignorance under which they function. In such a society as ours, therefore, those matters become open for general enquiry and discussion which were once hidden behind the curtain of shame. Not 'guilt' — for no one ever thought that human biology was somehow *wrong*, though popular ignorance is sometimes prepared to credit that view to 'the Victorians' — but 'shame', because they were private, and belonged apart from the public gaze. Questions about human biology are – in Saint Paul's phrase – to do with our 'unseemly parts'. The kind of discussion which we are now engaged in is itself a forcible example of the compelling need which our generation feels to expose the 'unseemly' to public view. But we will not understand our modern compulsion if we think of it as mere prurience on the one hand, or as merely being 'sensible' on the other. Our need to expose is motivated by our need to get a control of ourselves, which we do through experimental knowledge. To achieve the goal of freedom, we objectify ourselves; we take our biology from being that which we *live*, to be that which we *observe*, and so to be that which we *conquer*. This is the way of human self-transcendence that is proposed to us within a liberal scientific culture.

Let me pause for a moment on that phrase 'human self-transcendence' and try to clarify what is meant by it, for I believe it offers a key to understanding why embryo manipulation is more than a simple accident which has befallen us. 'Transcendence' traditionally defines the mastery of spirit over matter, and of God over both spirit and matter. A philosophy which proposes transcendence is, in some manner, a philosophy of spirit. It inherits the perspective of classical idealism, which relates man to the realm of spirit and subordinates the material world (including his own body) as an object of his use to higher, i.e. spiritual ends. In a scientific culture it is by making things the object of *experimental knowledge* that we assert our transcendence over them. It is popularly said of our culture that it is a materialist culture which ignores the whole dimension of the spiritual; and there is an obvious truth in this, in that experimental science conceives all knowledge on the model of our knowledge of material things, and treats only that which is susceptible of experiment and measurement as open to our knowledge. But the converse of this scientific conception of the knowable world is the universal scope of knowledge itself, as that which transcends the world of the knowable and does not belong to it. Spirit has not absented itself from our culture. It has merely withdrawn from the picture in order to come round, as it were, behind the camera. Spirit is present as the universal subject of scientific knowledge, as 'science' itself; and the very fact that it has no place in the picture as object, is a potent demonstration of how committed we are to the use of knowledge as a way of transcendence.

Mankind — to pursue our metaphor — is situated on both sides of the camera. He is studied object, and he is studying subject; he is of the world of matter, and participates in the spirit of knowledge. He can replace the kind of knowledge, of universe and self, which belongs to him naturally from his place *within* the system, by an experimental knowledge of self which puts him *outside and above* the system. That he should do this, rising above himself and distancing himself from what he is, appears to him to be the way of self-transformation which will fulfil his destiny by making him other than what he began by being. But in order to study himself at all, man must be differentiated, spirit and matter. Yet precisely that differentiation defeats the project of self-transcendence. We confront a paradox: we cannot pin ourselves down *in toto*, spirit and matter; we cannot see ourselves whole, because in the very act of seeing ourselves, a part of us is withdrawn from study. If we were to accept that a science of man should be confined to the study of his physical constitution, then there would be little problem; since our own material nature is already objective to us in a degree. But if we try to overcome this limit on the science of man, and make his behaviour, his freedom, his knowledge itself the object of scientific enquiry, then we seem doomed to chase our tails. How can we corner the elusive spirit, which declines to be an object of scientific enquiry as such? Only, perhaps, by studying a material correlate of spirit in man's physical constitution, by tying spirit down to its material substrate where we can examine it in a way that will assert our transcendence over it. This, I suppose, is the fascination of investigating the brain.

Embryo-experimentation takes its place naturally within

a programme of scientific self-transcendence such as I have just sketchily described. (And here I repeat a warning from a previous lecture: I do not pretend to describe the thinking or motivation of those who actually engage in such research. No doubt they are concerned simply with the compassionate goal of helping childless women have children. I am attempting to give some picture of the wider cultural assumptions which encourage and accept this research within our midst.) The embryo is of interest to us because it is human; it is 'ourselves'. On the other hand, it is considered a suitable object of experiment because it is *not* like us in every important way. It has no 'personality'. It is us and not us. In those two assertions we see the movement of self-transcendence taking shape. The embryo is humanity in a form that is especially open to our pinning it down as scientific object and distancing ourselves from it in transcendent knowledge. What makes this so suitable is that it is, we believe, undifferentiated humanity, in which spirit has not yet risen out of matter, personality has not yet emerged from its biological substrate. In the embryo, therefore, we have humanity *totally* present, before spirit has escaped from the material object in which it can be observed. We would not find embryos half so interesting if we believed either that they were already personalities (and so as difficult to observe as any human personality) or that they did not in some sense contain personality within themselves in germinal form. We should not imagine that because we deny that the embryo has personality, it is therefore not personality that we are interested in when we study it. On the contrary, only the embryo can make personality available to research, because only there is personality still undifferentiated from matter, present in its genetic potential (which can be mastered and measured) rather than in its elusive spiritual maturity.

For this reason embryo-experimentation looks like a natural and necessary practice for our civilization to adopt. It was not necessary, I suppose, that the embryos used for research should have been fertilized *in vitro*, but it is certainly appropriate. It is appropriate, for reasons that I outlined in my first lecture, that the occasion for such a project of self-mastery should be provided by the undertakings of compassion. It is also appropriate to the enterprise of self-mastery itself that the 'human subject' of these researches should be called into existence by us apart from any human love, precisely for this end of being mastered and explored, and so should stand from the beginning beyond the reach of our compassion, simply at our disposal. I do not wish to complain that this 'human subject' is really all the time a person, because I think (for reasons that must now be apparent) that both such a claim and its denial are in principle undemonstrable. It is enough to point out that the *ambiguity* of the status of the embryo research subject is precisely what is intended. It is what the task of self-transcendence needs, that it should be ourselves and yet not ourselves. If we should wish to charge our own generation with crimes against humanity because of the practice of this experimental research, I would suggest that the crime should not be the old-fashioned crime of killing babies, but the new and subtle crime of making babies to be ambiguously human, of presenting to us members of our own species who are doubtfully proper objects of compassion and love. The practice of producing embryos by IVF with the intention of exploiting their special status for use in research is the clearest possible demonstration of the principle that when we start making human beings we necessarily stop loving them; that that which is made rather than begotten becomes something that we have at our disposal, not someone with whom we can engage in brotherly fellowship.

I conclude, as in previous chapters, with a Christian confession of faith. It should, perhaps, take as its text Saint Paul's aphorism, 'Knowledge puffs up, love builds up' (1 Cor. 8: 1). I do not believe that self-transcendence by experimental knowledge is a proper goal of human existence. It is not 'humane' — in the true sense of that word, which is not: something that is fit to be done to human beings, but: something that is fit for human beings to do. It is not humane for us to attempt to alienate ourselves from ourselves and become other than ourselves. God calls us through the resurrection of Jesus Christ (which was a vindication of man's physical being, not merely of spiritual transcendence) to become precisely what he made us to be. I do not therefore believe that the correct mode of humane self-knowledge is experimental transcendence. To know one another as persons we must adopt a different mode of knowledge which is based on brotherly love. This implies a commitment in advance to treat all human beings as persons, even when their personal qualities have not yet become manifest to us; because there is no road which leads us from observation first to fellowship second, only a road which leads us from fellowship first to discernment second. It is said of God, by the same apostle and in the same place, that he has called those things that 'are not' to bring to nothing the things that 'are' (1 Cor. 1: 28). Unless we approach new human beings, including those whose humanity is ambiguous and uncertain to us, with the expectancy and hope that we shall discern how God has called them out of nothing into personal being, then I do not see how we shall ever learn to love another human being at all.

5. IN A GLASS DARKLY

Let me begin with a fairy-tale. Once upon a time there lived in a forest a woodman and his wife, who longed for children and had none. One morning as she sat grieving over the loneliness of her home, the goodwife was surprised by a sudden apparition. A majestic and queenly figure stood in her kitchen, clothed from head to foot in glittering white and bearing a sparkling silver wand in her hand. 'I am your fairy godmother', she announced. 'I have come to propose a sensible solution to your difficulties.' The difficulties, she explained, had to do with an occluded oviduct; and what she proposed was what we in our world call *in vitro* fertilization with embryo replacement, except that in place of the length, difficulty, and uncertainty of the procedure which we know, all was to be made simple and certain by means of the magic wand. The woman responded to the plan with joy, and had no difficulty in persuading her husband to co-operate. Everything was done as the magic visitor proposed, and then she disappeared on her way to help some other needy godchildren, leaving the woodman and his wife to cope as best they might in the heart of the forest with an unexpected but far from unwelcome pregnancy.

And the story goes on to tell, with more candour than is usual in fairy-tales, that after she had gone the worthy pair began to question doubtfully, and to wonder at the ambiguity which attends all our encounters with the supernatural. Was the blessing so strangely bestowed upon them not qualified by a certain unwholesomeness, by that air of the disreputable which always clings to the practice of magic, try as we may to deny it, like a slight odour of decay? And was their visitor, unquestionably generous as her intentions were, not altogether too practical and busy a person to have acquired that simple translucent virtue which distinguishes the fairy godmother from the witch?

In consenting to her plan, had they consented to something barbarous? and would they gain a child only to mourn the loss of their innocence — the very innocence which made them cherish the hope of children in the first place? Let us, while remaining strictly within the terms of the fairy-story, and without presuming as yet to discuss what may take place in our less picturesque world, ask ourselves the questions which might have perplexed the woodman and his wife. Consider some of the doubts which could reasonably have occurred to them.

1. The first doubt, perhaps, would not have caused them prolonged anxiety. They might have thought that this procedure savoured of black magic rather than white because it did not *cure* the tubal blockage which was the cause of infertility, but merely *circumvented* it. That is to say: this magic strove to become compensatory rather than curative medicine. We have already confronted this question in discussing gamete donation; and we maintained that although compensatory medicine has less immediate claim upon our sympathies than curative medicine, there is no objection to it in principle. In the actual world the secondary status of compensatory medicine may properly have negative implications for IVF in a competition for scarce resources; but in a fairy-story we assume that magic is an unlimited resource. It does not constitute an argument against the practice as such. It might, however, raise a second doubt. . .

2. Why was it necessary to adopt a compensatory approach to tubal infertility, instead of a curative one? Magic, after all, like scientific research, must be assumed to know no limits. If the fairy godmother had only concentrated her spells on the task of oviduct reconstruction, would she not have been able to cure the problem at source? Must we, then, not attribute her fascination with little glass phials to a more sinister interest in projects of a frankly necromantic kind? To such a doubt we must concede this much justification at least: if at any time there was a straight choice to be made between two approaches to a problem, equally likely to be effective, one curative and one compensatory,

it would be highly improper not to choose the cure, even if the other course offered gains for research not easily attainable otherwise. But the layman cannot judge whether this has ever been so, or could be so, with respect to oviduct reconstruction and *in vitro* fertilization. We should certainly not be in a hurry to assume that our scientific magic is capable of doing anything it sets its mind to. Failure to perfect techniques of oviduct reconstruction, which at present are limited, does not necessarily demonstrate a lack of will. There are, in fact, some striking examples of projects in this general field which have been assiduously pursued for some time with little success. And perhaps there is no need for the pious storyteller to attribute omnicompetence to magic spells in fairy-tales either.

3. To be taken more seriously is a third doubt: that childlessness itself is not a pathological condition, and is therefore not suitable for medical magic, whether curative or compensatory. We should not employ medical means to compensate for non-medical disappointments. If I am too short to join the police force, too quickly winded to be selected for the Olympic team, or too forgetful to pass history examinations, it is not a matter for my doctor to deal with. Unless, that is, my failures are manifestly related to some physical pathology (I used to remember dates all right until I had glandular fever), or so exceptional as to place me right outside the normal conditions of healthy existence (I am so short of breath that I cannot stand up from my chair), and so constituting a pathology themselves.

Now, the difficulty with childlessness is that it is a matter of chance whether a child is conceived on any one occasion or not. It is possible in principle for a couple to remain childless for a long time without anything being wrong with either of them. We should object to the idea that medicine may be invoked to overcome simple contingency, especially in the begetting of children, where contingency, as I shall argue shortly, plays an important role. Furthermore, the variations in fertility between one person and another, or between different periods in one person's life, are not simply to be ironed out into a maximal norm; they are valuable and appropriate to us as a race, and contribute to our natural differentiation and diversification. We should object to the idea that medicine may be invoked merely to enhance fertility. Nevertheless, it is clearly the case that childlessness arises, among other ways, from pathologies. Tubal occlusion is an example of this. An organ which is incompetent to do what it is meant to do is *ipso facto* pathological, and a proper object of medical concern. So, then, when it is said that childlessness is not a pathological condition and should not be treated as though it were, we may agree, but with this proviso; that though childlessness as such is not a direct object of medical attention, a pathology underlying it may well be, and medicine may attempt to compensate for that pathology as well as cure it.

The appropriate question to raise (leaving our fairy godmother for the moment) is whether those who practice IVF techniques are alert to the distinction between pathological and merely contingent childlessness; and here, it would seem, there may be some ground for dissatisfaction. The category of 'idiopathic infertility' is used to embrace cases of a persistent failure to conceive where there is no obvious explanation of any kind, and it is commonly defined in terms of two years without conception in the absence of evidence of abnormal semen or tubal deficiency. This categorization itself is open to the charge of treating contingency as though it were pathology. The difficulty arises from the use of statistics to determine a failure to conceive as pathological. Statistics may, of course, have a perfectly proper role to play in defining pathological conditions. They will provide appropriate criteria, for example, to define male oligospermia: when a particular ˙man has a quite abnormally low count of spermatozoa in the semen, then we are justified in thinking of his condition as a kind of pathology: his semen is no less manifestly incompetent to perform the task that it is meant for than a woman's blocked oviduct. But in the matter of achieving a pregnancy, statistics should be used with more caution. Pregnancy is not a condition of health, it is an event which depends on contingencies. It may be that a couple's stubborn childlessness is so abnormal statistically that the physician legitimately suspects a pathology which he cannot diagnose. But to suspect a pathology is not to prove one; and to dignify the case with the title 'idiopathic infertility' is merely to conceal the fact that it is the absence of an evident pathology rather than the presence of one that is puzzling. You cannot have a pathology which does not *belong* to either of the couple, but hovers between them, as it were, irresolutely. Although statistical abnormalities may entitle one to suspect a pathology, they do not entitle one to rule out the possibility that simple contingency alone is responsible. And in the 15 per cent of cases in which pregnancy follows 'spontaneously', that is probably the truth of the matter. We would have every reason to object, then, if IVF were generally invoked to deal with 'idiopathic infertility'. We understand that this is not generally done at present — though not for any such scruples as we have just expressed.[1]

4. A fourth doubt may assail the woodman and his wife, arising from the third. Granted that *in vitro* fertilization intends to treat pathology and not contingency, does it not have the effect of abolishing the contingency at the same time as it compensates for the pathology? If this is so, there will be a strong ground of objection to it (one which will not apply in the same way to some other means of compensating for infertility, such as artificial insemination). For the element of chance is one of the factors which most distinguish the act of begetting from the act of technique. In allowing something to randomness, we confess that, though we might, from a purely technical point of view, direct events, it is beyond our competence to direct them well. We commit ourselves to divine providence because we have reached the point at which we know we

[1] J. F. Leeton and A. O. Trounson, in Edwards and Purdy, op. cit. pp. 325 ff.

must stop making, and simply be. To say 'randomness', of course, is not to say 'providence'. Randomness is the inscrutable face which providence turns to us when we cannot trace its ways or guess its purpose. To accept that face is to accept that we cannot plan for the best as God plans for the best, and that we cannot read his plans before the day he declares them. There are, to be sure, ways in which we reduce the degree of unpredictability indirectly, by choosing the time of intercourse carefully, for example, to fit in with natural rhythms of fertility. Yet for all that we may encourage conception to take place, its occurrence is not the direct object of our technique. We do not, in natural begetting, bring sperm and ovum together, and, as it were, forcibly introduce them to each other. Thus we distinguish the act of begetting from those other acts in which we attempt to control the outcome directly, mastering with our hands or with their implements the material resistance which stands between the will and its proposed artefact.

But it is not the case that conception by *in vitro* fertilization abolishes contingency. It is true that it does so at one point: the actual fertilization of the ovum by the sperm is made the direct object of technique. There is therefore more difference between *in vitro* and *in vivo* than the mere difference of location that those phrases may suggest: there is a new, technical relationship to an event which has hitherto been subject only to indirect influences. But what is lost to contingency at the point of *fertilization* is not lost, but may even be enhanced, at the point of *implantation*. Implantation is still unpredictable and unmanipulable, an event which can only be encouraged, and not yet directly managed.

As one might expect, this very factor, which in our view goes some way to saving the humanity of the whole undertaking, is regarded by its practitioners as a technical imperfection to be overcome as soon as suitable means can be found. Since the early days of the practice it has been customary to reduce the element of unpredictability by replacing not one, but two or even three embryos in the womb, to increase the chance that one of them will implant. It is at least arguable that this does no further injury to the others than that which they might suffer in the course of nature anyway, for the fate of every new conceptus is doubtful. But it does reduce the doubtfulness which must attach to every *act* of embryo-replacement. It is easy to see why, from the administrative point of view, it is desirable to minimise the contingencies and maximise the rate of success at first attempt. Time, patience and resources are all consumed in repeated attempts which could be avoided. Yet this observation, while making the practice of multiple replacement intelligible, does so in a way that rather strengthens than mitigates the force of the case against it; for it is precisely the integration of human fertilization into the general demands of an administrative system that more than anything else confirms its status as an act of 'making' rather than of 'begetting'. We pointed our in Chapter 1 that the primary characteristic of a technological society is not the things it may *do* with the aid of machines, but the way it *thinks* of everything it does as a kind of mechanical production. Once begetting is acknowledged to be under the laws of time and motion efficiency, then its absorption into the world of productive technique is complete. The laws of operation cease to be the laws of natural procreation, aided discreetly by technical assistance; they become the laws of production, which swallow up all that is natural into their own world of artifice. That is why I think there is a great deal of symbolic importance in resisting multiple replacement of embryos. We should expect the practitioners to act inefficiently at this point, just as we expect researchers to act inefficiently when they are dealing with human subjects. Inefficiency is the worship they pay to the *humanum*, the human person and personal relationships, objects which cannot be subject to the laws which govern productive efficiency.

5. With this we come to the fifth doubt, which is the

most serious of all the doubts which might assail our fairy-tale couple and demands the most protracted attention.

In my earlier discussions of transsexual surgery and gamete-donation I attempted to show that the issue of the making or begetting of children is correlated to another issue, the unity or separation of the procreative and relational goods of marriage. I argued that when procreation is not bound to the relational union established by the sexual bond, it becomes a chosen 'project' of the couple rather than a natural development of their common life. Sexual relationship, correspondingly, loses the seriousness which belongs to it because of our common need for a generation of children, and degenerates into merely a form of play. The document submitted to the Warnock Commission by the Catholic Bishops' Joint Committee on Bio-ethical Issues has made this point the basis of its objections to *in vitro* fertilization, and has argued the case with great eloquence.[2]

If in. the course of natural procreation, the Committee maintain, the parents' hope for a child is fulfilled, then 'the child will be a gift embodying the parents' acts of personal . . . involvement with each other. Procreation will thus have been an extension of the parents' whole common life' (para. 21). But the same cannot be said of the child born as a result of *in vitro* fertilization, who will tend to be assigned 'to the same status as other objects of acquisition. The technical skills and decisions of the child's makers will have produced, they hope, a good product, a desirable acquisition' (para. 27). Although good parents 'will strive to assign the child his or her true status . . . they will be labouring against the real structure of the decisive choices and against the deep symbolism of all that was done to bring their child into being'. The 'structure of the decisive choices': that is what makes the decisive difference in the view of the Catholic Bishops' Committee.

[2] *In Vitro Fertilization: Morality and Public Policy* (Catholic Information Services, 1983).

In procreation by sexual intercourse *one and the same act of choice* made by each spouse governs *both* the experienced and expressive sexual union *and* the procreation of the child. There is one intentional act. . . . But in IVF there are irreducibly separate acts of choice, all indispensible, and all the independent acts of different people. . . . Thus the IVF child comes into existence, not as a gift supervening on an act expressive of marital union . . . but rather in the manner of a product of a making (and indeed, typically, as the end-product of a process managed and carried out by persons other than his parents) [para. 24] .

Within this argument we may notice two features. One is the principle that I have maintained, that procreation is safeguarded from degeneration by springing from a sexual relationship in which the child is not the immediate object of attention. The other is the further stipulation that these twin goods of marriage must be held together in *one intentional act* of sexual intercourse. The complaint against IVF is that there are 'separate acts of choice', that the unity of the procreative and the relational goods is not maintained in each single act. Now, it might seem that this further stipulation is merely a necessary clarification of what was implied in my principle. For the unity of procreative and relational goods will certainly be an empty thing if there is not some concrete expression of it. Anyone can agree, after all, that marriage should have both a relational good and a procreative one — and then pursue the two so distinctly that they become quite unrelated projects. And what other concrete point of unity can there be than the act of sexual intercourse, of its nature both procreative and relational? It is natural to assume, therefore, that the criticism of 'separate acts' maintained by the Catholic Bishops' Committee is the necessary corollary to our common concern.

Once we accept the 'one intentional act', however, certain other practices as well as IVF must fall under our disapproval. The Committee points out that their criticism applies also to Artificial Insemination (not simply to donor insemination, that is, which may be disapproved of quite apart from this doctrine, simply on the grounds of donor involvement, but to Artificial Insemination using the husband's semen). It does not say that their criticism could also apply to artificial contraception, which (in the eyes of some) is the Magna Carta of our modern separation of procreative and relational goods. There is nothing sinister about the document's silence on this point; indeed, it could be said to be the most responsible procedure in such a document not to raise issues which divide Christians, and indeed divide Catholics, if it is not germane to do so. In fact, the position maintained in the document does not necessarily imply a disapproval of artificial contraception, though it must tend to encourage such a disapproval. In the first place, the Committee explicitly denies that it objects to artificial intervention as such, and even suggests artificial procedures which would aid the act of intercourse to achieve its procreative goal without separating the acts. In the second place, it maintains the doctrine of the unity of the acts only to the point of saying that there must be no act with a procreative goal which does not also have a relational goal; it does not assert that there must be no intercourse for relationship alone without a procreative intent.

So, then, I mention contraception not in the mean and clever spirit of someone who thinks he has unmasked a hidden agenda in this Catholic document, but for two rather better reasons. Firstly, and incidentally, I wish to refute those who argue that the whole principle of the unity of relation and procreation was given away when we admitted artificial contraception. If even the Catholic Bishops can formulate the principle in a way that leaves the matter of contraception open, then the issue must be much more subtle than such objectors have supposed. Secondly, and more importantly, I mention it because there is an aspect of the contraception debate which affords an illuminating parallel for the question in hand. One of the arguments in favour of artificial contraception which Paul VI's famous encyclical mentioned, but did not answer, was that which he described as 'the principle of totality', that is to say, the principle that the sexual life of a married couple should be viewed as a whole, not in terms of its distinct acts of intercourse. Fornication may take the form of a series of one-night stands (for that is its moral corruption, that the sexual act never leads beyond the occasion to establish a permanent bond of loyalty), but married love is entirely different. To break marriage down into a series of disconnected sexual acts is to falsify its true nature. As a whole, then, the married love of any couple should (barring serious reasons to the contrary) be both relation-building and procreative; the two ends of marriage are held together in the life of sexual partnership which the couple live together. But it is artificial to insist, as *Humanae Vitae* did, that 'each and every marriage act' must express the two goods equally. What was at issue in the matter of contraception was not the unity of procreation and relation as such, but the Moral Theological tradition known as 'strict act-analysis', which tends, in the eyes of its critics, to atomize certain human activities in ways that defy their inner structure.

Here, too, in the Catholics' argument against IVF, we have an instance of 'strict act-analysis'. They argue that the offensiveness of IVF and AIH resides in the 'irreducibly separate acts of choice . . . the independent acts of different people', by which the IVF procedure is carried through. To which we may reply that there are *distinct* acts of choice, which involve persons other than the couple, in any form of aided conception, including those forms of which the document approves. Whether they are *independent* acts of choice is precisely the question which requires moral insight. If they are indeed independent (and not subordinate to the couple's quest for fruitfulness in their sexual embrace) then they are certainly offensive. But that point cannot be settled simply by asserting that they are distinct. The question remains: is there a moral unity which holds together what happens at the hospital with what happens at home in bed? Can these procedures be understood appropriately as the couple's search for help within their sexual union (the total life-union of their bodies, that is, not a single sexual act)? And I have to confess that I do not see why not. News reports tell us that some IVF practitioners advise their Roman Catholic patients to have sexual intercourse following embryo-replacement, in order to respect the teachings of their church. It would seem to me that such advice might well be given to all patients, in order to help them form a correct view of what is, or should be, meant by the technique: not the making of a baby apart from the sexual embrace, but the aiding of the sexual embrace to achieve its proper goal of fruitfulness. Something of this kind, perhaps, is intended by another document submitted to the Warnock Commission, that from the Nationwide Festival of Light, which adds to its general approval of IVF and AIH when practised simply to aid childless marriages the caution: 'It should be stressed that we would envisage married couples continuing to enjoy normal sexual relations throughout their married life, despite the need for "assisted conception" techniques.' It should be stressed indeed, and not simply as a romantic afterthought, as though to suggest that the relationship may continue undisturbed while procreative enterprise proceeds in different ways, but as a fundamental point of reference which alone can make the procedure morally intelligible.

It may, of course, be wondered whether such subtleties are beyond the understanding of most couples who participate in the IVF programme, and whether such a practice can only have the effect of enforcing the widespread view of procreation as a project of the will. It may even be thought that the cultural influence of the practice is likely to be so bad that IVF should be discouraged for that reason alone. To such a suggestion perhaps we are in no position to put up a strong resistance. After all, the experience with contraception makes it highly plausible. It is possible that a wise society would understand IVF as a temptation; it is possible that a strong-willed society would resolve to put such a temptation aside. But this takes us beyond the scope of our fairy-tale, in which no cultural consequences need be feared. These cultural questions are different from the question of whether there is something intrinsically disordered about IVF. And to that question we have not found reason (speaking simply, of course, of IVF as practised by fairy-godmothers in fairy-tales) to return a negative answer.

What, then, was achieved by discussing a fairy-tale? It enabled us to concentrate our attention on an ideal, hypothetical simple-case IVF pregnancy, and so evaluate the procedure in the abstract. That is an important step in the moral discussion, but not one at which we can stop. Many current discussions seem content to stop there; but if we are to evaluate IVF as it really is, and not as it might be in a world of magic wands, we must take account of certain contextual features which are inseparable from it in reality. I shall speak of two such features in particular, which I think to be of central importance.

In the first place there is the inextricable involvement of clinical *in vitro* fertilization with non-clinical research on early human embryos. I say 'inextricable' although I am aware that some practitioners in this field insist on keeping these two questions distinct (as, of course, in conceptual abstraction they are). And I do not undervalue the restraint which some practitioners exercise in their research activities precisely in order to commend their work on its merits as clinical practice. Nevertheless, the distinction between this clinical practice and the research which supports it cannot be maintained with much plausibility for very long. We may accept two simple statements of fact from Dr. R. G. Edwards: 'Oocytes and embryos were grown during . . . early investigations without intention of replacing them in the uterus'; and: 'This preliminary period is by no means completed, even in hospitals and clinics where many pregnancies have already been established by IVF. Improved methods are needed to assess the normality of growth of the embryos, and to sustain or monitor their development without impairing the development of those which are to be replaced in the mother'.[3] In other words: IVF did depend on non-clinical embryo-research in order to become established; and it still does depend on non-clinical embryo-research in order to perfect its techniques. IVF is not the gift of a fairy-godmother; it is the gift of researchers. The suggestion that we can thank these researchers for their gift, make use of what they have achieved, and simultaneously declare all their research, past and future, to be illegitimate, is strikingly lacking both in consistency and realism. Our view of IVF, then, is necessarily determined by our view of non-clinical research on early embryos.

The second feature is the risk to the child who will be born; and in raising this issue it is necessary to specify rather carefully what kind of risk we are talking about and what its moral significance is. There may, in the first place, be risks of genetic or other defects which already arise in the course of natural procreation and which are replicated in artificial procreation. We may expect children born of IVF to show the same proportion of defects as children born in the course of nature; and such an event need not trouble us. There may, in the second place, be an *enhanced* risk of such defects, which is *indirectly* attributable to the IVF procedure. We may fear that more children may be born with inherited defects because the natural process of selection through foetal wastage is inhibited by the measures taken to ensure replacement. This will certainly trouble us, if it should turn out to be the case; but to what extent it will appear to be a decisive consideration will depend, no doubt, on the extent of the increment by which the natural risk is enhanced. It will be a matter of prudential judgement to decide whether this increment is compensated for by the great good of circumventing childlessness. I am speaking now about neither of these kinds of risk, but about risk *directly* attributable to the IVF procedure itself. Will there arise defects which are due,

---

[3] Edwards and Purdy, op. cit. p. 372.

not to natural risk, not to the enhancement of natural risk indirectly, but directly to the procedure itself?

I do not claim to know, or even to suspect, the answer to that question. As I understand the situation, nobody knows the answer to it with certainty, even now. B. A. Liebermann and P. Dyer write of the 'as yet undetermined incidence of chromosomal and other diagnosable defects peculiar to *in vitro* fertilization'.[4] Experience with embryos frozen for a long period before replacement is still very limited. But even if somebody does now know the answer, or suspects that he knows it, and even if that answer is as favourable to IVF as could be hoped, it is still the case that nobody knew the answer when the procedure was inaugurated. And it is *the willingness to take these risks*, rather than the favourableness or unfavourableness of the outcome, which in my view gives its most decisive characterization to the whole enterprise.

The risk is usually justified by an argument that runs something like this: since there are risks associated with natural conception (which in some cases can be very high), why should we be more reluctant to incur risks from artificial conception than we are to incur those? Thus H. W. Jones maintains: 'This argument [i.e. the argument against risk-taking] could equally well be applied to a couple, the female of which is above the age of 35, where the expectation of an abnormality is measurable.'[5] And Gerald Elfstrom: 'Natural conception entails its attendant risks for the unborn without offering any clearcut benefit to it.'[6] We must not confuse this reply with another, which sounds very similar and, as I have said, raises no problems. It does not mean that artificial conception merely reproduces risks already attendant on natural conception. It means that we must be prepared to take new risks, uniquely related to artificial conception, because we have hitherto been prepared to take old risks related to natural conception. The

---

[4] in Edwards and Purdy, p. 335.
[5] Edwards and Purdy, p. 354.
[6] *Hastings Center Report* 9 (2) p. 4.

logic of the argument, it seems to me, is that we must lose all sense of difference between nature and artifice, between the constraints which are given to us as natural conditions for our lives, and the liabilities of projects which we have freely undertaken and might as freely not have undertaken. Thus Elfstrom revealingly concludes his argument: 'Both kinds of event [i.e. defective births arising from natural and artificial causes] result from human actions, and therefore both kinds of risk to the unborn may be avoided by human restraint.' That is the conclusion to which a technological society must certainly come. Even natural procreation is something which we may equally well undertake or not undertake, and it is subject to exactly the same cost–benefit calculus which we apply to all our projects. Thus having children 'naturally' is just another instrumental means chosen to realize a project which could, if it proved more efficient, equally well be realized by technical means. The whole of life, as I argued in the first lecture, comes to be interpreted in the light of technique.

We are faced with a choice, as Paul Ramsey rightly said in his reply to Elfstrom, in which 'no one can long halt between two opinions: one favouring artificiality as more human, delivering us from the "necessities" of nature, the other favouring the spontaneities of natural procreation'.[7] Like the people of Israel we must choose between Baal and Yahweh: but is it between the Baal of nature and the Yahweh of artifice (as an older generation of Old Testament critic liked to suggest) or between the Baal who may be manipulated by magic and the Yahweh who is sovereign Lord of man and creation? That, perhaps, is the fundamental form of our question. For the appearance of neutrality is only an appearance. Once we begin to justify the risks of artifice by analogy with the uncertainties of nature, we have put ourselves in a masterful position *vis-à-vis* the natural processes. The first step for any man to take in the understanding of divine providence, is to comprehend that

[7] Ibid., p. 21.

God has evils at his disposal which he does not put at ours. Though he works good through war, death, disease, famine, and cruelty, it is not given to us to deploy these mysterious alchemies in the hope that we may bring forth good from them. There is the world of difference between accepting the risk of a disabled child (where that risk is imposed upon us by nature) and ourselves imposing that risk in pursuit of our own purposes.

As we began with a fairy-story, so let us end with a futuristic fable, set in the Europe of the twenty-first century, a Europe revolutionized by the diligent activities of the European Court of Human Rights. There were two persons disabled from birth, Jack and Jill, one born in the course of nature, the other as a result of *in vitro* fertilization. And it happened that when they reached years of discretion, the charitable society which was responsible for their support took the usual steps on their behalf. That is to say, it initiated wrongful-life suits against their parents, which was the customary means by which the society funded its charitable work out of the pockets of the parents' Insurance Companies. Jack accordingly filed his suit, charging his parents with negligence in omitting the usual precaution of amniocentesis and abortion, which would have spared him the curse of life and consciousness. Jill, however, proved unwilling to go along with what was asked of her. She said she loved her parents and did not want to sue them; and although it was explained many times that this was purely a legal and administrative matter which implied no breach of personal relationships, she stuck to her guns. Finally, when her charitable guardians pleaded with her that the care of such as she could never be funded if such sentimental feelings were always to be indulged, she proposed a compromise. She would do the unheard of thing, and sue the doctors responsible for her fertilization, alleging that her defects were due to IVF. And so it happened, to the consternation of the medical world and the pleasurable excitement of the legal one.

Of Jack you would hear no more, if it had not happened

that his case was heard by a quixotic and idiosyncratic judge, one of those conservative old men of extensive antiquarian culture and a dislike of modern ways who do occasionally crop up in the legal profession though not as often as rumour would have it. And he dismissed what should have been a straightforward wrongful-life suit, invoking arguments that had been popular back in the twentieth century when such practices were strange and unfamiliar. He ruled that no one can sue for injury who is dependent upon the alleged injury for his standing to sue. Life is the presupposition of our ability to do anything else; therefore 'wrongful life' is a contradiction in terms, because a wrong can only be done to someone who already has life. One can sue one's mother he declared, for injuries sustained in the womb: one can sue her for smoking or drinking or taking drugs or driving without a seatbelt. But one cannot sue her either for conceiving one in the first place or for failing to terminate one's existence after one is conceived. And here he quoted some words from the ancient Book of Isaiah: 'Will the babe say to his father, "What are you begetting?" or to his mother, "What are you bringing to birth?"' (45: 10). The parents of a child, the learned judge continued, were not responsible at law for the conferring of life upon the child in the same way that they might be responsible for other actions they performed. The law traditionally took the view that strictly speaking the ultimate author of a human life was not a parent, but a person or force that could not be made a defendant in court. It was altogether a paradoxical decision, and it would have remained a curiosity of the legal histories, struck down at the first opportunity by the appropriate review tribunal, had not a startling event occurred to perpetuate it.

That event was as follows: Jill's case came forward, and was heard by a judge of entirely modern sympathies, a lady of great subtlety and some wit, who immediately perceived the usefulness of the judgement in *Jack v. N and M* and used it as a precedent to dismiss Jill's case against her doctors. It had been elegantly demonstrated, she said, that one could not sue for wrongful life because life was the presupposition of the standing to sue. The learned judge had said, moreover, that the author of life cannot be made a defendant in any court. But in this case the medical team quite clearly occupied the position traditionally assigned to the author of life, by virtue of their having conferred existence upon the plaintiff *in vitro*. The argument, therefore, which protects the parent from prosecution for wrongful life, protects IVF doctors *a fortiori*. No one can sue the author of her existence; and if the parents, as relative authors, were thus protected, how much more the ultimate authors by whose acts existence is immediately conferred? And with exquisite appropriateness the judge concluded her judgement by capping the older judge's quotation with the words that come immediately before it: 'Will the pot contend with the potter, or the earthenware with the hand that shapes it? Will the clay ask the potter what he is making? or his handiwork say to him "You have no skill"?'

Can we resist this reasoning? Can we deny that risks taken in relation to a child's conception are risks for which the child can never properly hold anyone responsible? Can we deny, therefore, that the IVF practitioner, who takes these risks, not as a parent does, in renunciation to divine providence, but in calculation relating to his technical project, places himself in a quite unparalleled position *vis-à-vis* another human being? Is there another instance in our moral experience where someone may, in pursuit of a scheme of world-betterment, impose injuries upon another human being for which he cannot subsequently be held responsible? These paradoxes arise only because the beginning of a human being has come to be at the same time also a making; and that transformation has occurred, not, in my opinion, as a result of the separation of acts, but as a result of the taking of risks which place those who take them above the interrogation of those who suffer from them. I confess that I do not know how to think of an IVF child except (in some unclear but inescapable sense) as the *creature* of the doctors who assisted at her conception —

which means, also, of the society to which the doctor belongs and for whom he acts.

If anyone finds this conception grotesque and self-evidently wrong, I congratulate him on his good habits of thought — but with a warning. Good habits of thought teach us to find the notion of one human being as the creature of another odd and repulsive; but habit alone will not protect a culture against the 'paradigm shift' in its perceptions which will occur when too much in what it observes and does is more obviously thought of in a new way. If our habits of thought continue to instruct us that the IVF child is radically equal to the doctors who produced her, then that is good — for the time being. But if we do not live and act in accordance with such conceptions, and if society welcomes more and more institutions and practices which implicitly deny them, then they will soon appear to be merely sentimental, the tatters and shreds which remind us of how we used once to clothe the world with intelligibility.

For myself, I do not *believe* that the doctor has become the child's creator. I do not believe it, though, as I have admitted, I do not know how to reconcile my unbelief with the obvious significance of *in vitro* fertilization. I can only confess, as a matter of Christian faith, that I believe in another and unique Creator who will not relinquish to others his place as the maker and preserver of mankind. To those who wish to make this confession with me let me put this closing question: should we not expect that a humanity which is so made will vindicate its maker, and his creatures, against every false claim to lordship?

INDEX

Index